Everyone is unique, yet the same.

We have all won, yet we know loss.

We know love,
and we know heartbreak.

We are the sum of our experiences
but we do not let them define us.

How?

By rediscovering our joy
and pursuing our passion.

The byproduct?

Everyone thrives.

How cool is that?

Ready to rediscover *your* joy?

FindUniquelyU.com

Uniquely U. Update #52

The Birth of a Bright-Eyed Entrepreneur

Written by

Angela DiMarco

Phenom PUBLISHING

First printing in the U.S.A. in 2022 by

𝆏
Phenom
PUBLISHING

A DIVISION OF THE UNIQUELY U. GROUP LLC
NEW YORK, NEW YORK

Cover artwork "Joshua" painted by Dana Sardano, Copyright © 2022
Cover and interior design by Angela DiMarco © 2022

First Edition 2022

ISBN 979-8-9872105-5-0

Foreward

As the Editor-in-Chief of Phenom Publishing, I have had the unique opportunity to edit this written work by my dear friend, Angela DiMarco. Not only was this experience special because we are collaborative business partners and friends but also because I got to witness and experience firsthand this book being written *as* it was being written.

Every week, I'd read each update as it came through in real time. I was privy to all the back stories that were the catalyst for each email, while being incredibly involved both emotionally and energetically to the experiences that brought forth these communal messages. I was gifted such a rare and beautiful opportunity to witness someone, who I hold so, so very dear, through the creation of her incredibly courageous business endeavor, evolve into the best version of herself.

I've witnessed Angela weep, and I've joined her in celebration. I've observed her avoid the discomfort as well as faithfully leap into the unknown—then leap again, and again, and again, as I gleefully cheered her on as she skillfully landed on the other side—every...single...time. I've seen her get dirty and fearlessly go public with it, and I've witnessed her withstand the naysayers and critics as she stood proud in each of her accomplishments. I have watched Angela release fear and shame as well as self-sabotage and self-deprecation and transmute it into love and joy and peace and freedom, and while recovering from these feats of courage and resilience, create a foundation for others to do the same.

For what presently is two years since her first update, I was privy to the front lines, had seats on the 50-yard line, sat center stage, was invited backstage, and flashed my VIP pass every chance I got so as to experience the most intimate moments with this beautiful mind. I was privy to all of it, and to see what came out the other side was such a gift to me—a gift to all of us.

So, having read Update #52 in its entirety and having relived all of it in one stream of consciousness was quite a profound experience for me as I presume it will be for you. Together we will witness that bubbly (sometimes rudderless) 18-year-old Sigma Delta Tau pledge that was reintroduced to me in the fall of 2020 evolve into the magnificent creature that stands before us today. In these updates, Angela reveals herself without inhibition. We see her humanness, feel her joy, her love, her kindness. We sense the palpability of her sensitivity, her care for others, and her desire to help them succeed. We can feel her angst and the insecurity of her inner child holding on for dear life as her warrior spirit takes over with fierce determination. Our mouths will collectively fall agape as the emergence of her innate ability and ingenuity through her perseverance and drive become more evident with every written word.

These 52 updates are a true window into the evolution of

Angela's soul and each update gives us a greater glimpse into her star power and creative genius. Without waxing too poetic, all I can say, as I reflect with such immense admiration, is watch out world because the Angela DiMarco that stands before you today IS a full-fledged fucking phenom.

Dana Sardano
Co-founder/Editor-in-Chief
Phenom Publishing

Co-founder/Chief Officer of Content + Curriculum
FindUniquelyU.com

Gallery Owner / Resident Artist
Ubuntu Fish Gallery

Published Author
- *Ten Recommandments for Personal Empowerment*
- *Beyond the Ten, Decoding the Woo Woo*
- *Veda Finds Her Crown*
- *Soul Traveler Cards of Empowerment*
 (in collaboration with Ann Marie Skordy)

Facebook Post

December 4, 2019

"Babies lost in the womb
were never touched by fear.
They were never cold.
Never hungry.
Never alone and importantly,
always knew love."

~ Anonymous

Saddest news ever...we lost our little boy yesterday at 2:15pm—I was 18.5 weeks along. He just wasn't cooked enough to survive. We are at peace, accepting that this was God's will, that something was so wrong with our little angel that he would have likely lived a very hard life. Dave was my rock as we went through the miscarriage, and the staff at Stony Brook University Hospital was amazing. Dave, Mattie, (Christian) and I are just very sad. Our son Joshua will always be in our family's heart. If you've been through this, please message me. I could use some guidance as we cope with the loss.

#miscarriagesupport #miscarriage

This leg of my journey is dedicated
to my angel baby Joshua.

Prologue

Amidst the despair of losing my third child on December 3, 2019, I began to question everything—my spirituality, my career, my hope, my faith—EVERYTHING. As I recovered from the grief, I embarked on a fact-finding mission to figure out my purpose.

I found Aaron Doughty on YouTube—an adorable, young guy who shared his knowledge of the workings of the universe and spirituality and awakening. I would listen to his short videos as I drove to work, and I would be like, *Yes, I get that! Me too!*, but then I'd have no one to talk to about the concepts that I was feeling so drawn to—the 'woo woo' stuff, if you will.

Occasionally, his friend Victor Oddo would pop up, and eventually I started to pick up what *he* was putting down as well, but still, not having people to talk to about it all was frustrating and limiting. And just like that, as if the universe knew what I needed, (doesn't it always?) in August 2020, a 3-month-long online 'ascension' workshop that Victor was running came into my awareness. I signed up for it immediately.

This virtual workshop (to this day I can't remember what he actually called it!) took place every Sunday from 12–2pm EST throughout August, September and October. I had never done anything like this before, but I just had so many questions and needed SOMEONE to talk to!

To set the stage, during that summer into the fall of 2020, my family was living in a small, two-bedroom apartment while we were saving money to buy a house. My 10th grade daughter was schooling from home because of the Covid-19 lockdown, and I was working my 8am–4pm-er from home with her. My two-year-old son was still able to go to daycare, and my husband's chimney business was considered essential, so he was not around most days.

Considering the circumstances and tight quarters, sacrificing two hours on a Sunday, my only day with the family together, and confining myself to one of the *three* living spaces in our apartment was a difficult ask, but something in me needed it, even if I didn't fully understand how much at the time. My family was helpful and understanding; though, they had *no* idea what the heck it was that I was doing.

In any event, the workshop was great. Victor generously shared his experiences and knowledge, and he facilitated eye-opening exercises that put a lot of pieces of the puzzle in place for me. I also made amazing friends from all around the world and looked forward to our Sundays together.

In one exercise, we had to look back on previous ages of ourselves and remember what we wanted to be when we grew up. I think it was like ages 5, 13, and 21 (give or take a couple years).

At age 5, I wanted to be an artist or a teacher.

At 13, I wanted to be a doctor.

At 21, I wanted to finally connect with Eddie Vedder, lead singer of Pearl Jam, and be such great friends that he and the band would stop by for a home-cooked meal and jam session when they were in town for a show. So specific, I know! Silly 21-year-old me!

Well, that particular Sunday night, Dana Sardano, my Sigma Delta Tau pledge mom from University of South Florida back in 1992, who I absolutely adored and who you will be getting to know very well as this story unfolds, randomly sent me a link through Messenger for a contest to meet Eddie Vedder.

Besides the occasional interaction on Facebook and a lovely message after I lost Joshua, we really hadn't been in personal contact, so the coincidence of this was not lost on me. I told her this, and it opened a dialogue between us. Dana, an artist, had a beautiful painting style that really resonated with me, so I asked her if she would be willing to paint a painting of me and my three kids as we are today. We worked out the payment details, and I sent her a sketch and then a couple weeks later, she sent me the completed painting of me and my three children. It exceeded all my expectations and was a perfect tribute to my angel baby.

As our ascension group was coming to a close, during our last few sessions, Victor was guiding us towards figuring out our purpose. I had this idea that I jotted in a notebook for an online education/collaboration/community platform that was similar to what Victor offered plus hints of other online platforms that already existed but with an added human connection component that I couldn't seem to find anywhere. It was totally lofty, and it felt impossible, but at the same time, so possible and *so* necessary.

By mid-November 2020, after the Trump/Biden presidency debacle and while Covid was getting annoyingly political, I was beginning to feel stuck once again, so I booked a virtual intuitive guidance session with Dana, a service that she provided out of her gallery. This would be the first time I saw her since 1993.

When she came on the zoom call, I'll admit that I got all fan-girly, and it took me a good five minutes to catch my breath. It might as well have been Eddie Vedder himself! We did the catch-up thing, and then we did that whole *I told her what's happening in my life, and she gave me her insights* thing, and it was fun and laid back. Towards the end of the session, Dana asked if I had any other questions, and I asked if I could read her my idea.

After I sheepishly read my idea to her, she paused, and then said, "huh." I began to close my notebook, embarrassed for even attempting to have such a lofty idea, when Dana continued with zero hesitation, "That idea is PURE Gold! You *have* to see that through!"

From that day on, we spoke on the phone every single day, so much so that Dana made a joke that "Ya pay for one intuitive guidance session, you get the next 300 free!"

Now the wheels were turning! By December 3, 2020, just one year after losing Joshua, I incorporated Uniquely U., bought the URL FindUniquelyU.com, and created a business email address. And by January 1, 2021, I was working on the business plan and gathering up the earliest supporters for what was to be the most rewarding, challenging, and enlightening journey of a bright-eyed, first-time entrepreneur.*

I hope you enjoy this peek into my window.

*Some names have been changed in order to protect people's privacy.

"Joshua" by Dana Sardano

36" x 36" — Acrylic on Canvas

Find U. Crew — Weekly Update #1

Sent: Thu, Jan 28, 2021, at 3:02 PM

What's up, my high vibe tribe!

Weekly Communications

I think it is important to the momentum of this project to stay connected, so I just wanted to give you an update on where things are. I will attempt to send you updates like this on a weekly basis to help keep me accountable. As we go along, I will be adding trustworthy insiders to this list. This week, I would like to introduce you all to my soul sister and fellow weirdo, Dana Sardano. She is the spark that lit this fire and continues to fan to the flames. And she is awesome and highly intuitive and a kickass artist and friend.

Beta Workshop #1

I am securing an office space to host the first workshop series on brand foundation development. It will be on Tuesday evenings (somewhere between 6–9pm EST) to start, and I may add one on a Sunday afternoon (somewhere between 1–4pm EST), depending on interest and availability.

I still have to write up the course description and plan the workshops, and figure out the tech, so aiming to start Feb 9th or Feb 16th. More details to come as they unfold. Hopefully you can join!

Beta Workshop #2 or Video Lecture Series #1

Jules, are you still interested in running a workshop or video series? The latter would be great content for our marketing goals if you are more comfortable with that. Let's chat this weekend some time!

April Showers—gonna make it RAIN dolla bills, y'all!

Dave and I are booking our flights to Las Vegas. Will be there April 26–April 29 (conference is Tues–Thurs, we leave Thursday at 11:05 pm). I will be accepting this award and promoting the shit out of Find U. My goal is to have the business plan, the team and vendors ready to go, because that will be the point where we go public with the idea, we start looking for money and we prepare to get to work!

Uniquely AND You.

As I said on the call last week, if you feel called to work with this business in any capacity, there will always be a place for you. I've already talked to Charlie and he is on board to play an important role in helping to guide people and help them get excited about their future. Email me and let me know what you feel compelled to do with the business, and we will work it into the plan. I am counting on Chit's resume and interviewing workshops to be a staple in our offering, but I do think Chit has so much more to offer as do each of you! I can't wait to watch all of you shine so brightly that I'll need to wear shades. :)

Have a great day, my dear friends!

Angela

Find U. Crew — Weekly Update #2

Sent: Fri, Feb 5, 2021, at 10:07 AM

Hello, my beautiful companions!

Welcome Aboard!

This week, we have three new crew members! Please help me welcome dear friends of Dana—Wendy, Raina and Michelle! These amazing women will be joining us for the Brand DNA workshop, and I am so excited to get to know them! Also, I've added my little peanut Mattie to our crew, as she is the biggest fan and supporter and future of this company. Her insights are truly beyond her years! I'm also cc-ing Dave and my family, even though they didn't ask to be included, because they are along for this ride whether they like it or not!

Vegas, Baby!

Our flights are booked. Our hotel is almost booked. And I have been writing my acceptance speech in my head. For our new friends, I am receiving a *Top 100 Leaders in Marketing & Advertising* award at the MARsum World conference in April. It's kind of a 'smoke-up-the-butt' situation to sell tickets to this seminar, but it did spark this whole thing, so I am using it to launch Find U. I'll give a 1 min. acceptance speech that will be live-streamed, and I'll be interviewed by local TV—all assets we can use to make Find U. seem more legit!

Course Descriptions

I absolutely LOVE how excited so many of you are to teach workshops! Your ideas are truly inspired and will bring out all the best that Find U. has to offer. I ask that you take my course description below and use that as an outline for your workshops and video lecture series. Nothing is set in stone, so no pressure, but I need to have a catalog of courses to show investors that we are serious, and we are ready! The only requirement is that you focus on helping people find their unique aspect in whatever you are teaching. I will hopefully demonstrate this in the beta Brand DNA workshop, and those of you who were in Victor Oddo's coaching group will already have a grasp on this. Please email me course descriptions over the next couple of weeks. I'll remind you, don't worry!

Beta Video

Jules is wrapping up a really interesting video about being fully present. When she sends it to me, I'll get it hosted and will send a link for your viewing (and surveying afterwards) pleasure!

Beta Workshop

I have visited two spaces that I can rent for the workshop and am seeing one more this coming weekend. For now, we are still on deck to host the first one on 2/16. If I find myself procrastinating, I will move it back to start 2/23. Please let me know if you want to join, or if you have friends who would be interested.

- - - - - - - - - - - - - - - - - - - -

Find Uniquely U. Online Workshop Series

Course Title: **Brand Development Part 1: Brand DNA– Decoding your "U" Chromosome**

Instructor: **Angela DiMarco,** *Brand Navigator + Find Uniquely U. Founder*

Duration: **1 hour +30 min open forum per class, 4 classes**

Schedule: **Night Owls: Tuesday Evenings, 7pm-8:30pm EST — 2/16/21, 2/23/21, 3/2/21, 3/9/21 (20 students)**

Location: *A meeting link will be sent to you with your registration confirmation.*

Course Description: Your brand is reflected in all you do and say. Every action either elevates or denigrates your brand, so let's dive in to truly understand who you are and what you stand for. In this course, you are going to define all that makes you uniquely tick by going underneath the surface to unearth your differentiating qualities. Don't worry, it'll be a fun process! This course is ideal for those who wish to develop their personal brand (perfect for job hunters), those starting up a new business or are currently running a business that could use a reboot, and anyone who wishes to learn this process. There will be roughly 1 hour of homework between each class.

Required:

- Computer (with camera and mic) is preferred but a smartphone will work.

- Good internet connection.

- A handy dandy notebook.

- Participate with a positive attitude and an open heart.

- (Suggestion) Block this time off your calendar so you can participate without interruption. This is YOUR time. Enjoy it!

This course is worth 4 completion credits towards your Find U. Score.*

This is a feature that will be live when we launch and your credits will automatically be applied to your profile. For more info about this, contact Angela.

About your instructor: Angela has been branding companies large and small for nearly 20 years. She is passionate about making corporate-level branding guidance accessible to everyone. To get to know her better, find Angela on LinkedIn, Facebook, Instagram, Twitter or preview her portfolio.

- - - - - - - - - - - - - - - - - - -

This Is Our Playground

One thing I really want to reiterate is that this business will never be corporat-y, stuffy, or riddled with anxiety. We are building this to help people shine their bright, beautiful light. If you feel stressed about anything regarding Find U., let's talk. You are here with me for a reason, and I want to ensure that every minute of your experience with this is positive and beautiful so your light be-comes a beacon for those we need to reach.

That is all for this week! Thank you for being U.

Uniquely Yours,
Angela

Find U. Crew — Weekly Update #3

Sent: Thurs, Feb 11, 2021, at 10:17 AM

Hello All!

Welcome Aboard!

Please welcome our latest high vibe crew members Noah and Sally! Noah is a captain and Sally (my gorgeous aunt) owns a local beauty salon. They both will be joining the workshop and my weekly updates.

Brand DNA Workshop

I am super excited about the workshop—planned it out, and it is going to be fun! If you want to join us on Tuesday nights starting 2/23 at 7pm EST, let me know!

What the heck is Find U. all about?

For all our new friends, I can set up a call to walk you through the business concept. Maybe we can do it Tuesday Feb 16th, so I can test out the Wi-Fi and setup in the space I will be conducting the workshop. Let me know if you are interested and available next Tuesday at around 7:30pm. You can email me privately if you are interested.

My Status

I have an idea of how I want to put together the business plan for this. I'll be working on it over the next month or so, pulling in partners and filling in the blanks, so we are ready to rock with it in April and start looking for money! Any ideas or suggestions along the way are greatly appreciated! I've accounted for those of you who have expressed interest in areas, whether it be teaching a workshop or running a part of the business. I guess more will be revealed to all of us as it unfolds!!

That's all for this week. Keeping it short and sweet this time (you're welcome! Ha ha ha)

Uniquely Yours,
Angela

Find Uniquely U. Weekly Update #4

Sent: Tues, Feb 16, 2021, at 6:52 AM

Good morning!

I've been "advised" to get my ass started early, before the chaos of the day job and family kick in. So here I sit at my dark kitchen table drinking my MUDWTR and writing to you.

Business "Hello!" Pages

I find this business to be like an octopus—so many exciting arms all working to support the big picture. One of these arms will be our business listings. Find U. is all about creating opportunity. We encourage our instructors to sell their products and services, and we support our students' success. As our community grows, this directory of businesses will expand and cover just about anything you could need!

Since our platform is not developed yet, I've added our community's "Hello!" Page links to our Facebook Group. Let me know if you wish to be added/removed. No rules. Whatever you want to promote for yourself, however many links, it's all good! Let me know if you have a little one-liner about your business that you would like included (for those in the workshop, we will be writing yours.) I just ask that you consider clicking around and utilizing a service that speaks to you when the time is right.

Brand DNA Workshop

I'm busy preparing for our beta Brand DNA workshop starting next week, Tuesday Feb. 23rd at 7pm! We have 14 participants in all different situations, guaranteeing a truly unique experience for all! I will be sharing the replay link in my weekly email for those who can't attend the live workshop. I have room for maybe two more participants, should anyone else still want to sign up.

Getting down to business (and keeping me accountable)...

As some of you know, I have decided to cancel our trip to Las Vegas, declining the award. MARsum was moved to the end of June (due to Covid), and it simply didn't resonate as being the right opportunity for us anymore. The award served its purpose to help spark this exciting adventure, so for that I am grateful!

That being said, I am still shooting for mid-April to have the business plan and pre-launch marketing campaign ready to go. As I develop the plan, roles in the business will become clearer and we can start to tangibly dig in and prepare for launch as soon as we get funded.

Since the money planning part is not my forte, any leads to someone who can guide me here would be greatly appreciated!

Do you have any information about *Common.is* or *Sphir.o*? Both are platforms I am looking into for our business.

Well, my MUDWTR is finished, and my official morning is about to begin. But before I sign off, I just want to thank each and every one of you for your enthusiasm and support of this project. This business is not mine. It is ours. I have a vision for it, but I am open to ideas on how to make it as amazing as I think it can be. And the joy of this journey is getting to know new, brilliant, wonderful people and connect with old friends. Thank you, from the depths of my heart, for being here with us. You are important. Your input matters. And I appreciate you!

Uniquely Yours,

Angela

PS - Dana, you were right...again...mornings are kinda awesome to get things done. Mwah!

Find Uniquely U. Weekly Update #5

Sent: Wed, Feb 24, 2021, at 6:33 AM

___

Good morning, my friends!

It's 6am, and I sit here with my cup of MUDWTR, just reeling from last night's (first) beta workshop! I am beyond grateful for all who participated and shared. If you haven't yet, please join our Facebook group and connect and collaborate with each other. And if you have any feedback from last night's session, please do not hesitate to send it my way, so we can address any issues for the next meeting. After all, that's what beta-ing is all about, right?

As I lugged my bag of equipment to and from the little travel agency office that I am renting from a super sweet couple for $20/hour, this class honestly made this whole business concept feel REAL. I am so pumped (well, as pumped as I can be at 6am) and so ready to dive into the next steps to bring this more to life!

I have to shape this, and maybe Ivy can help (hehe), but last night I discovered our brand purpose:

With real human connections, we will light up people inside and provide opportunities to set their world on fire!

Thank you again for being you, for being here and for being AWESOME!

Uniquely Yours,

Angela

Find Uniquely U. Weekly Update #6

Sent: Fri, Mar 5, 2021, at 6:00 AM

Good morning, friends!

I am just now getting the time to write you all a little update. It's been a very busy week!

The Book of Face

If you haven't already, please join our private Facebook group, where we connect, collaborate, and jam to daily tunes by DJ Charlie! You may invite friends and colleagues to join the group who you think would dig our little business model and who would be fun members of our community. *(Facebook is most likely a temporary solution, as when this thing launches, I will have a proprietary social platform that is more in line with our core values.)*

Beta Brand DNA Workshop

Class #2 is in the can! I am learning so much about this concept through this one little class. I can't thank the participants enough for their willingness to learn something new, for their honest feedback and for their optimism. It really puts some pep in my step, so thank you! The replay link and homework were sent out to all who registered for the class or expressed interest in the link. If you did not receive it or would like to be on that micro list, reply and let me know. It's free for all who want it.

Crazy little thing called love...

Self-love and self-care are so important for the soul. It has been brought to my attention that I may be one who gives so much to others, and it is time for me to give MYSELF some time for me. These 5am wake-ups are starting to be a welcome change in my routine—and that's crazy talk because I LOVE sleeping in—for I take a few minutes upon awakening and just sit in the quiet with myself. I mull over my bizarro dreams to see if there were any insights provided, and I just breathe...and then I turn to my laptop to write to you all and work on the next workshop before Mom's Diner opens and the morning rush starts. I'll ask in the Facebook Group for strategies folks have for some good self-lovin' and self-care? I'm new to this whole thing!

That being said, I'm doing my first FOR ME thing, and I'm stoked! I'll be heading down to celebrate Dana Sardano's first children's book *Veda Finds Her Crown* at Chakra-Con! I will be in Florida for less than 24 hours, but to be able to fly down and celebrate my girl's awesome, AWESOME accomplishment, it is worth it. See you Floridians on March 20th (my brother's birthday AND the first day of spring!)

Business listings are posted in the Facebook Group. Please let me know if you would like yours updated or if you would like to add a one-liner about your offering so that we can start sharing the love and utilizing your services.

That's all for today. Make today fantastic and do something special just for you today...

Uniquely Yours,
Angela

Find Uniquely U. Weekly Update #7

Sent: Wed, Mar 10, 2021, at 1:40 PM

Good afternoon, Find U. Friends!

I just want to welcome all the new folks to my little email ramblings. Thank you so much for joining us! If you have any questions, please do not hesitate to reach out to me.

The Brand DNA Beta Workshop

We just completed our third class last night. It is SO cool to see those of you participating get something out of this that you find valuable and useful! The insights I am gleaning from this experience are right on point and proof that this business concept is going to work, so thank you!

New FREE content coming soon!

The lovely and talented Jules has put together a beta video presentation that we will be setting up for your viewing (and surveying!) pleasure in the coming week! This will be to beta test another function of Find Uniquely U. More on that to come...

Are you a LinkedIn pro?

I am looking for someone to help me with some LinkedIn stuff. If you are an avid user and would like to represent Find Uniquely U., please let me know. I pay in hugs and feel goods (super valuable these days!) Ha! Seriously, though, I can't let the day job see me have any activity in this realm, hence why I need a front man.

Come on in, the water's fine!

If you know of anyone who would benefit from what we are building here, please ask them to join us. You can send them to FindUniquelyU.com (it will be updated as time permits) or to our on Facebook group (the devil! LOL)

It is super important for the future of this business to grow our community. Facebook has this fancy marketing device called a 'Lookalike-Audience' that builds a targeted audience based on your best customers (for lack of a better word). So please help spread the word and help bring your friends into the fold! Find Uniquely U. 2022 thanks you!

So what's shiz with the biz?

I've reached out to a video production company to help put together a promo video for us. I will be interviewed by our resident 'Oprah' Dana Sardano, and we will be pulling footage from the Brand DNA workshop. This asset, along with the business plan (that I will begin working on next week), will be the tools to help us find the cash to get this party started (woot woot!) By the end of April, we will start the hunt.

And speaking of businesses, please utilize the "Hello" Page Business Listings in our Facebook Group for whatever you may need. If you would like to be added, just let me know!

CHAKRA-CON!!!

O.M.G.! I am so excited to be in Florida for like 18 hours to celebrate my girl Dana's AMAZING accomplishment. She wrote the first book of her children's book series, and we are celebrating her awesomeness! Learn about and buy the book (available at the time of this writing at Phenom-Publishing.com /Dana-Sardano) I can't wait to see all my peeps next weekend!!!

Lately, I've been saying this mantra..."*I am letting go of things that no longer serve me.*" It doesn't mean that I am severing relationships, but rather, pulling back emotionally. It means that I am focusing solely on the things that bring me joy. I am taking a bird's eye view of my reactions to life and changing them to BETTER serve me (how can I handle this situation that may be uncomfortable in the most joyful way?)—I have to say, it is liberating! So, I leave you with this question:

What can you let go of today that no longer serves you?

Uniquely Yours,
Angela

Find Uniquely U. Weekly Update #8

Sent: Fri, Mar 19, 2021, at 9:54 AM

Hello friends,

I must admit, this has been a pretty draining week. I've been exhausted and just taking some much needed mental downtime; hence, this email is coming to you on a Friday morning.

The Beta Brand DNA Workshop was an enormous success!

My intention was to grab some good Zoom footage and sound bites for a promo video and hopefully provide a little bit of useful information. And, while my underlying real intention was to prove out the Find Uniquely U. platform, I had little expectations because we 'only' had about 15 participants.

But man, was I blown out of the water on this! This experience with these amazing people was beyond extraordinary! So much so that my drive to get this going has shifted into 5th gear! EVERY SINGLE REASON why I want to create this platform was proven in just four workshop sessions. Connections and friends were made. Businesses were utilized. Personal insights were gained and sparks were ignited!

I want to build this platform so that the party never has to end! New friends can take new workshops together or meet at in-person or virtual events. People who have a desire to coach and teach will have a platform and an audience to do so, and do so on their own schedule.

Find Uniquely U. will be a place for good vibes only.

I kept saying this in the workshop—there will be no room for assholes here! We will learn from and with each other, sharing all the nuggets we've gained from life's lessons and experience-es. We will support each other to grow in our businesses and personal journeys.

At the end of the day, we all want the same thing. Freedom. Whether that means making bank so you can buy nice things that bring you joy or having a business that allows you to live a laptop lifestyle and travel or just making just enough so you never have to WORRY about bills.

This is what Find U. offers everyone—golden opportunities to live your definition of freedom.

So, you can see, I HAVE to build this for us. But I am going to need some help...

My next steps are to write a highly detailed business plan so we can go out for startup funds. With the understanding of all I said above, *can you recommend someone who can work with me on the logistics/business side of this thing?* I need to whiteboard this out with someone experienced with building a community/service-based, online platform. I have revenue models and projections in mind at a high level, but since I've never built anything like this before, I could use a pro to tap in. Feel free to forward this email to anyone you think might be a good match. Thank you in advance!

And I am still looking for a LinkedIn Ambassador. Reply if this piques your curiosity!

Survey Says!

If you would like to learn more about the Find U. business concept, I'm considering putting together a live webinar or pre-recorded video. If you are interested, please respond to the survey posted in our Facebook group—if you are not on FB, then reply to this email and let me know which works for you:

1. I'd join a live webinar to learn more on a Tuesday 6pm EST.
2. I'd join a live webinar to learn more on a Sunday 2pm EST.
3. I prefer to watch a pre-recorded video.

CHAKRA-CON — Here I come!

I am flying down to celebrate Dana Sardano's first children's book *Veda Finds Her Crown* and see all my amazing friends!! If you don't live close and can't make it, go online, and purchase her book and swag and support this inspiring creator!

Thanks for being a part of this. Enjoy your first day of spring this weekend!

Uniquely Yours,

Angela

There is no Update #9...

...because I miscounted once I started numbering the updates (I was obviously a bit less organized than I am these days in 2023)! It's funny to look back on how this weekly email evolved without a plan or structure. I was simply following my intuition to connect with those who expressed interest and support.

Let's get on with the show, shall we?

Find Uniquely U. Weekly Update #10

Sent: Thurs, Mar 25, 2021, at 12:15 AM

Well, my friends...shit is getting real! Apologies in advance for the lengthy email but so much is happening!

For the new people (hi!), I use this weekly email to keep myself accountable as I create this business for us. This is truly a start-up/entrepreneurial adventure and when it is a global phenomenon, we will look back at these early emails and say, "Holy crap, remember when...?"

As most of you know, I took a quick trip down to Stuart, Florida this past weekend to celebrate my friend Dana's new children's book *Veda Finds Her Crown*, and I have to tell you...the clarity that came to me was like a playbook being handed to me. I understand the revenue model and projections for Find U., how everyone can make money by teaching workshops and most importantly, how FEASIBLE this is!

YES, there are a ton of moving parts. YES, this is a gigantic undertaking. YES, it will cost a lot of money to build it. But, most importantly, YES, I have complete faith that it will work, and it will help so, so many people around the world connect and find their joy.

There are a few very important things that have been set in motion this week:

I am meeting with two web development companies to get estimates on building this platform. It is probably the biggest portion of the investment dollars we will be hunting for, but it is really important to choose a partner that can build us a proprietary, scalable, cyber-safe platform. Both companies are located in Poland, and I am really excited to speak with them! (Ethnically speaking, I am a quarter Polish, so a little bit of my heart resides there.)

Another exciting thing is that we will be making the promo video soon using the footage from the Brand DNA Workshop (thank you again!) and Dana interviewing me. I really think this will be a very valuable and persuasive asset as we go off hunting for cashola. This will also help a lot of you who are newer to my ramblings to understand what this business really is all about. I am hesitant to put too much 'out there'. I will host a webinar where I can explain it live, and you can ask questions. I am just waiting for the right time to set that up.

I was just tinkering around on the website, beefing it up with some new brand copy that I received from an extremely talented friend who can make words magically delicious. It's funny...I was waiting to work on the business plan until after the beta Brand DNA Workshop was complete. The universe knew that if I had this great copy prior to completing the workshop that I would lose focus and want to work on both. Yet, divinely timed, I received it the weekend after our last session and read it on the plane going to see my beautiful friends in Stuart, and it lit me up like a Christmas tree!

Please share the link FindUniquelyU.com with your friends and colleagues to join this mailing list. We need to start gathering up potential students and getting our instructors lined up and ready to go. And everyone I talk to knows someone who would benefit from what we are building here, so bring them into the fold!

Facebook sucks, I know. But it is my necessary evil right now so I can reach as many people as possible. If you are a FB user, join our group. Start and engage in conversations. Share your pearls of wisdom with each other. I promise to build our own little, closed-campus social platform, but until then, we have to use the free tools that are at our disposal.

In closing, I just want to remind you that I am just winging this whole thing. I am doing this on my off hours around my day job (Sleep? Overrated!), and I am trusting my intuition and inner guidance. So far, it hasn't steered me wrong. And if this whole thing doesn't work, so what? I've met so many amazing people already. And it's been a blast to imagine a future reality where Find Uniquely U. unites a global community by freely sharing knowledge with the "soul" agenda to lift each other up so we can all live our definition of freedom...and it's SPECTACULAR! (any Seinfeld fans out there?!)

Uniquely Yours,

Angela

PS–If we haven't talked in a while, please drop me a line and say "hi!" and let me know how you're doing!

PSS–Hey Newbies! I'm curating our business, content, or portfolio links. Just a few are posted on Facebook (with no context yet—that is to come). If you would like to be added, please reply to this email with your link or channel so that our growing community can tap into your expert skillz! I'll be adding these to the website, but for now, we are grassroots!

Find Uniquely U. Weekly Update #11

Sent: Thurs, April 1, 2021, at 12:32 AM

Hello Friends! How are U all doing out there? I, for one, am moving right along and feeling super inspired and motivated! I have an exciting offer for you, but first...

This week in the adventure of starting-up a business.

I took some sage advice from my aunt and cashed in a PTO day with the day job so I could focus on Find U., and I made SO much progress!

- We welcomed a whole bunch of new people to our email list this week! Thank you for being here with us on this journey! You can always reply to my emails if you have any questions or would like to be removed from future emails. No hard feelings :)
- Two of eight parts of the business plan are written! Moving right along, folks!
- I've found a free business mentor through the SBA and have a meeting set with him on Monday (FREE! Best four-letter word for a new entrepreneur!)
- On the sage advice of my colleague to vet at least five partners, I have had two meetings already with web

development companies and three more on the calendar (this is no small feat, and we need some really big guns from the start.)

- I've received over 15 submissions for workshops from future Find Uniquely U. instructors! I know there are more of you who want to teach but have not yet filled out the description. Please take a moment to do so at FindUniquelyU.com. It can be high level, I just want to get ideas of our offering and populate the business plan thoroughly.

- The Brand DNA Beta Workshop survey is out, and participants have been submitting their answers (Thank you!!!) The testimonials are amazing and will be sprinkled throughout the business plan, so your time and your comments MATTER! I heart U all! If you haven't done so, please email me your biz app profiles and links for our Hello! Pages.

Okay, so what about that offer?

One of my dear friends and earliest Find Uniquely U. crew member (might even be the third person I shared this idea with along with Martha and Dana?) has graciously put together a Beta Video Presentation for your viewing and learning pleasure! See below for the content description and link/password. All I ask is that you provide your thoughts on the content and format (with little regard to the platform, because as you know, we are being scrappy right about now!) ENJOY!

- - - - - - - - - - - - - - - - - - - -

New, FREE **Find Uniquely U.** Beta Video Content

Video Title: **Full Body Presence**

Instructor: Jules Carter

Duration: 1 video about 50 minutes long

Schedule: On-Demand

Location: *(link no longer available)*

Course Description: Are you feeling stressed and burned out? Focusing too much on the past or future but not the present? Feeling anxious and worried? *Full Body Presence* provides tools that help you stay present and grounded in your body, listen more fully to your body's innate wisdom, and live more fully in the present moment. This course is ideal for those who wish to create a better connection with their body and cultivate mindfulness-based self-care strategies. Listen—your body is speaking to you! (This course may expand into five-mini courses to explore each principle more deeply.)

Required:

- Computer

- Good internet connection.

- A handy dandy notebook.

- Participate with a positive attitude and an open heart.

- (Suggestion) Block this time off your calendar so you can participate without interruption. This is YOUR time. Enjoy it!

About your instructor: Jules is a Certified Healing from the Core Practitioner and acupuncture student. As a bodyworker, she specializes in craniosacral therapy and stays up to date on the latest training in trauma-informed therapies. She is committed to creating a safe space for individuals, families and communities to heal.

- - - - - - - - - - - - - - - - - - - -

Please chat with us on Facebook and invite your friends to join our mailing list.

That wraps up this week's email blast. Remember to light up your day by staying present and grateful. **I heart U!**

Uniquely Yours,
Angela

Find Uniquely U. Weekly Update #12

Sent: Mon, April 5, 2021, at 11:35 AM

Recorded on 4/5/2021

Going to mix things up a bit for you all and try something new!

I just made this little Welcome Video for our new Facebook group members and thought I'd share it here. I really don't like making videos, but I am trying to step outside my comfort zone here!

TRANSCRIPTION: "Hey everybody. I am going to try this video thing. It's not my thing, but I have a lot of new members here in the group, and I want you guys who don't know me to start to get to know me. Welcome to Find Uniquely U.! There's a lot about this business that is not out there right now because we're in the development phases. I will be putting more information through my email because that's a little more secure, so if you guys want, go to FindUniquelyU.com and join my email list so that you can be a part of what's going on. I am coming to you from my son's play area because I am thinking today about how important it is to play and have fun and enjoy life. So, take time today to do something that brings you joy—doodle during a meeting, take a walk, breathe in the sunshine if it's sunny where you are, but just today, really enjoy something for yourself. This is a reminder for me too because I tend to just get a little crazy.

I'm going to try to do more of these little videos that you can get to know me, and I'll tell you what's going on with the business. I'll do more blog type stuff through email and the website.

But for now, exciting things are happening. Things are starting to just become real and it's really, really exciting, and I can't wait! We're making a brand video. We're talking to web dev companies. We're going to find some cash, and we're going to make this this platform for you guys to bring everybody together, and it's going to be awesome.

So, for now, if you need anything, if you have any questions, please talk to any of our crew. We've got Charlie here, who's amazing, Sarah, Dana, Michelle, Sally, Wendy. I can't even, there're so many awesome people here who are the original Find U. crew members. Chit even, I'm sorry if I didn't say your name because I just really feel weird about this whole video thing!

There's one thing I wanted to ask you guys about. I'm starting intermittent fasting. So, it is 10:30 here in the morning, and I haven't broken fast yet. But in between that time when you're fasting, water is okay right or no? Coffee with no sweetener, that's okay? If not just let me know if you have any ideas and good foods to eat like in that window—right now doing eight hours of eating because I'm not a glutton for punishment, and I want to have fun and play.

So let me know in the comments if you have any suggestions for intermittent fasting and how I can do this so that it becomes the right thing to do for my body. I just want to point out this beautiful painting behind me—got my kids with me—that's by Dana Sardano, and that's Joshua, Mattie, Christian, and I, and we're all here to tell you to go out and play. Okay, have a great day! It's nice to meet all of you. I'm Angela, Peace and Love."

If you happen to be on Facebook please join our group.

Watch the Beta Video

If you haven't yet, please enjoy this fascinating presentation on **Full Body Presence** by the lovely Jules!

This week in the Adventures of Starting Up a Business

Status quo—continuation of last week:
• Meeting with web developers
• Meeting with promo video maker
• Writing the business plan
• Meeting with the financial advisor/mentor
• Working with our future Find U. instructors!

Welcome to all the new folks who joined this list! I am humbled and grateful! Keeping it short and sweet this week (you're welcome!)

Happy Easter to all those who celebrated it!

Uniquely Yours,
Angela

Find Uniquely U. Weekly Update #13

Sent: Mon, April 12, 2021, at 2:23 PM

Hi Friends!

It has been a crazy busy week! I was up until 2:30am on Saturday night working on this document for an upcoming workshop with a web developer for our platform, and it was so much fun! I feel so accomplished and so proud of my work. If Christian hadn't come running to get me, I might've put in another hour or so!

I am dropping a screenshot here so you can see my *Beautiful Mind* work that I am really proud of! This is a list of all the awesome functionality I hope to build for y'all! (not meant to be read, just awed! Haha–giving myself an attagirl).

I've had a lot of opportunities to explain this business concept now to new people (our new video producer, several web dev companies pitching our business, a mentor, my husband...) If you're here and new to my emails (welcome!), I like to share my progress on starting up this business. And if you've been around for a while on sheer faith but have no idea what we are all about (thank you!), here is a brief overview on what FUU. is and who it is for.

In a nutshell, what is Find Uniquely U. all about?

Find Uniquely U. is designed to connect people through live virtual workshops led by instructors who are passionate about their offering. We are opening doors for people who may be starting up a business or heading on a new career path, or maybe they are just lonely and frustrated from this pandemic and want to safely connect with real people.

We're taking the best of what is out there (LinkedIn, Masterclass, Skillshare, Coursera, local networking groups, Clubhouse, Facebook, Craigslist, coaches, etc.) to create a really easy-to-use, fun, engaging, university-campus-style platform. It's extra online education-meets-networking-meets opportunities and good times for all!

Describe the Find Uniquely U. community.

Like yourself, the FUU. community are people you might start chatting with in a coffee shop or know from a church group.

Friends of friends from all walks of life. Our common thread is kindness and being open to discovering new things. From rough around the edges to shy to enlightened, we're commonly and passionately driven to learn, teach, and connect. We're the ones who like to have fun, who might not take life so seriously, who see the glass half full. Seekers, dreamers, make-it-happeners.

We inspire and lift each other up—ALWAYS up!

Who are the U-Instructors?

There are SO many people out there who are really, REALLY good at something and they enjoy sharing their nuggets of knowledge, but they may have no formal certification and/or do not know where to begin. They can start a business, but that is not easy. Find Uniquely U. provides the platform, the students, the marketing, and the opportunity to earn as much money as they want based on the time they want to put into it. We currently have 18 U-Instructors on deck!!

If you are interested in becoming a U-Instructor, please go to FindUniquelyU.com and fill out the application. This is totally informal and if you don't have the details just put 'To Come' in the required fields. I am going to put a video together getting deeper into this, and I will only be sending to those who have raised their hands expressing interest.

So that's this week's update. I LOVE receiving thoughts and comments back, so please don't be shy!

Make this a great week and do something that inspires you and ignites your passion.

Uniquely Yours,

Angela DiMarco, *Founder, CEO*

Find Uniquely U. Weekly Update #14

Sent: Tues, April 20, 2021, at 4:20 PM

Hello friends,

This has been an interesting week for me.

I tend to take 'direction' to the extreme, especially when it is to do something that will help me achieve a goal. Whether that guidance comes from a friend or my inner wisdom, it doesn't matter. I chase what feels good, and to the over-achiever in me, everything is exciting and everything must happen RIGHT NOW! (It's exhausting!)

So, this past week, I heeded the warning signs of some inconvenient consequences of my harried self (such as falling off my bike and busting my butt, dropping my laptop which thankfully didn't break), and I stopped everything. I focused on whatever task was in front of me and nothing else. I let everything else fall by the wayside. Between Dana, Michelle and my guides, I listened and reacted as I always do—to the extreme.

But you know what? In that extreme down time, I felt guilty and stressed. I felt like I was losing momentum with you guys and with the business. And there, in that uncomfortable feeling, the lesson was learned.

I can listen to solicited or unsolicited advice from whomever, but I don't need to respond, react or blindly 'do' immediately. Instead, I can say, "what serves me best at this moment?" I need to sharpen my discernment tool. I like to work in the mornings and at night, but when I feel my eyes start to get heavy, I need to call it quits and get rest. I enjoy multitasking—I feel connected and on the pulse of this business—but when I feel pulled in too many directions, I need to save tasks for another time.

I suppose this is my way of saying that maybe you all don't need a weekly email update from me. I don't think half of you read them anyway! We aren't in a place where it REALLY matters in the big picture of this platform. Not yet. But it will be soon and at that point, I'm going to need all the help I can to get this built.

Soon though—you AWESOME U-Instructors—I'll be ready for you! Together we will shape your courses and content, and you will help shape the very nature of this platform. In the meantime, I'm going to be head's down on this business plan and gathering my estimates on costs (the web dev stuff is SUPER exciting, and I can't wait to share with you!)

So, if you don't hear from me, reach out. I may not be able to chat on the phone, but I am always available via email or FB. Thank you to all of you who put the wind beneath my wings. Did you ever know that you're my hero?

Uniquely Yours,
Angela DiMarco, *Founder/CEO*

Find Uniquely U. Weekly Update #16 (no 15?!)

Sent: Wed, May 5, 2021, at 12:31 AM

> "Share the light, Won't hold us down."
>
> Lyrics from the song *River Cross* by Pearl Jam

Welcome to all the new folks who have signed up for these weekly updates! If you have any questions, please feel free to reply to this email.

For the entire month of May, my dear, talented friend Jules Carter is hosting a free, guided meditation every day at 7:30am PST (adjust to your time zone). All you have to do is click on the link to join the Zoom call *(no longer available)*. Jules is using this as an opportunity to practice leading meditations and to provide an opportunity for us to take time to center ourselves in the midst of our day. I've joined the past two days and it has been wonderful! Please join if you can so she can expand her wings. Hope to see you there!

This little business of mine...I'm gonna let it shine.

I'm going to begin sharing some details about this platform because I am so looking forward to it becoming real some day! Today I'd like to share a little bit about what it will be like to be a guest and a member of Uniquely U.niversity.

Guest Access: Any user will be able to create a free guest account and click around on the Campus Commons social feed (limited access) and shop in the U-Campus Store. They will have unlimited access to shop the Hello! Pages listings and solicit services offered by paid members. And they will be able to browse the content but will not be able to register for any workshops or view any videos from our library.

Guests will also be able to submit an application to be a U-Instructor, and once they pass through our vetting process, they'll have to purchase a membership before they can begin teaching (don't worry, earnings from just one workshop will likely more than cover an annual membership fee.)

Members With Benefits: $15.99/month (and subsequently discounted term packages) gets you unlimited access to the entire platform, including all the videos in our library and the opportunity to register for live workshops (for an additional fee that covers the U-Instructor's fees and operating costs.)

You'll receive a free listing in either the Hello! Pages directory for businesses or personal endeavors, or a product listing at the U-Campus Store, where you will also receive a 10% discount on all the products and school swag.

Members will also be able to interact with each other on the U-Social Network, submit U-Instructor endorsements, and join any group of interest, whether that be a particular school or topic within Uniquely U. or a U-Instructor's group and post con-tent wherever they choose.

Members who submit an application to be a U-Instructor will be made a priority over guests and will be fast-tracked through the vetting process.

With 20-student-max video conferencing workshops ranging from business and marketing coaching to healthy living, home improvements and even some metaphysical content, there is plenty of opportunity to get what you need while also discovering your passion within U.

~ Excerpt from the Business Plan

Let me know if this kind of info is interesting to you or if it is too granular. This is just a tiny, TINY piece of all that resides in my brain, and now partially in the Business Plan, of which I am slowly and steadily making progress on. I'm learning so much about myself through this process—like how to listen to my body and emotions. If I get all angsty, I need to find the source of that feeling, face and embrace it, make a choice on how I want to proceed based on my present circumstances, and move right along merrily down the stream. After all, life is but a dream, right?

Do you have any friends who would be interested in what Uniquely U. will offer? If so, please invite them to join the mail list. There will be perks for you early birds, I will do my best to hook you all up. My sole intention is to build this thing so you all can start doing YOUR thing! Like my spirit animal Eddie Vedder sings, "Share the light – won't hold US down!"

Thanks for reading! Until next week, stay magical, my friends!

Uniquely Yours,

Angela DiMarco, *Founder/CEO*

Find Uniquely U. Weekly Update #17

Sent: Wed, May 12, 2021, at 12:29 AM

**To all the moms, I hope you had a wonderful
Mother's Day celebration!**

My home team really made me feel special this year, but every day is special with this crew! My kids are magic, and Dave is my rock. This life I am living today is so much better than the daydreams I had about it 10, 15, 20 years ago. I am blessed beyond measure and driven to squeeze the most mother lovin' fun I can out of it, which brings me to the business...

Where in the world is Uniquely U.niversity?

As I was working on the business plan this past weekend, I realized that there are so many words I am writing...so many details that are going to make this platform the amazing, reliable, safe space to find our true selves that we all so desire. I was getting overwhelmed and I'm only six pages in! An idea came to me, and I discussed it with the smartest consultant I have on the payroll, my almost 16-year-old daughter Mattie. On Saturday night, we excitedly talked it through. On Sunday morning, while the boys were making me breakfast, I sketched it up. By Sunday night, I had the graphic created and I think it's gold, so I wanted to share!

I invite you to view the **Uniquely U.niversity** eCampus Map:

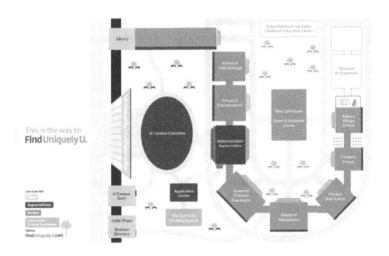

For those of you who have recently submitted forms for *amazing* courses, and even for those who did so weeks ago, I'll be reaching out in the near future to confirm your offerings so I can weave it into the business plan under the appropriate school. Once the plan is done and we are out hunting wabbits, I will be able to work with you a lot closer and we can begin to really curate and design your courses. We are still 4–6 months away from launching Uniquely U. I thank you for your patience, your enthusiasm and your contribution to our inevitable success!

If you are in our Facebook group, you know that one of my passions is songwriting and playing guitar. It terrifies me to play with anyone other than myself. I keep asking the universe to make it easy for me, so until the stars align (living room jam session with Eddie Vedder? Not yet? Okay, I'll wait, but really looking forward to it!), I will pick up my old Breedlove acoustic that might need to be put out to pasture soon—which is so sad, but the old girl can't hold a tune anymore (must be time for that 12-string Martin I've been eyeing!)

Today I had the urge to learn one of my favorite songs of all time. It'll take some time, but with practice, I'll get it down, and when I do, I'll record it for y'all because it makes me happy to play and sing and *screw you, fear!* My life is so full of love and gratitude that it's like rush hour on the train in Tokyo. Any remanences of fear are squished up in corners—still present but not so powerful with its face smashed up against the window.

This song could be the **Uniquely U.** anthem. It is so powerful, so simple, so profound.

"...where the speechless unite
in a silent accord
Using words you will find are strange
Mesmerized as they light the flame
Feel the new wind of change
on the wings of the night"

~ Lyrics from the song *On the Turning Away* by Pink Floyd

And with that, I bid you a good week ahead. Cherish each blessed moment, even the messy ones. We're here to have FUN! Thanks for reading!

Uniquely Yours,

Angela DiMarco, *Founder/CEO*

Someday

Song written by me, Angela DiMarco

It's okay baby, don't cry.
Time to say bye for today.
I'll see you tomorrow,
and we'll laugh and play.
I'm sorry that I can't change
our current situation.

But someday...someway...I have faith...

Please know you're all that I want.
This is not my choice,
to have you so far away,
but I'm getting stronger for us.
I believe that it's just temporary, baby.
We'll be together the way that we want.

Someday...some way...please have faith...

You are the light of my life,
my reason for breathing.
It's gonna be alright. Just give me a smile.

So much worry in those tiny shoes.

Whenever you need me, I will be there.

Remember there's a cord between us baby,

and it can never break

(and we'll be together I know it)

Someday...some way...let's have faith...

Good evening, friends,

Quick reminder that you are welcome to join my girl Jules's daily, 20–25 min grounding meditation at 7:30am PST. Please don't be shy—she is awesome, and it would be lovely to see some new faces!

As I was thinking about what to write in this week's update, this song I wrote a long time ago came to mind. This is for all the divorced parents out there who have or had to share their time with their kid because a relationship with the other parent went south. Having to leave my then 6-year-old with her dad and rest my head at night in my bed in another town was brutal.

But it was also transformative.

I realized that it would not have served any of us if I stayed in an abusive and miserable marriage. Instead of wallowing in self-pity, I harnessed the pain and worked through some really intense traumas that ruled my behaviors. I tended to the seeds on my side of the fence, and the byproduct was Ireland-green grass right under my feet! And consequently, I was able to mother my child as I saw fit. She had me all in, even when I wasn't physically with her.

See, prior to leaving the marriage, I was living an inauthentic life (almost typed 'lie' there, which is equally appropriate!) Having been a people-pleaser for most of my life, I had no clue who I was, what I liked, or needed. But the second Mattie was put on my chest in the delivery room, I knew in my heart of hearts that I was meant to be her mom. And that knowing changed everything.

I started to do things *I* wanted to do, things that were deemed "selfish" and "inconsiderate" and whatever else you can think someone would say when they too felt the shift and the anxiety of their reign over me coming to an end. Less than three years later, my bags were packed. The road to where I am now was long and treacherous, but I must say, the debris became easier and easier to move out of the way. The incline of the road began to level out, and the directions became clearer to follow (see where I am going with all of this metaphorical stuff?)

So, what does all that have to do with **Uniquely U.**, you ask?

At the very core, following through on this business concept is about me being authentically ME. Just like I knew I was meant to be Mattie's mom, when it comes to this business, I feel this... Understanding? Knowing? Intuition? Chutzpah? (Pick the word that resonates with you.)

No, I have not led an entrepreneurial life, but I know I am an entrepreneur. I've never, EVER written a business plan, but I have one about 75% finished and it is f-ing gold! I am forecasting the finances of this business like I was born with a calculator in hand (and my HS math grades were TERRIBLE!) It is innate, and the confidence I have in my vision and ability to see it through is palpable.

More than the concept of **Uniquely U.**, I believe in MYSELF. Why would I set myself, my family and my friends up for anything less than awesomesauceness? Failure simply isn't an option because no matter what happens, no matter how this plays out, there will be lessons learned and growth along the way, and that, my friends, is something that money simply can't buy. The only way is to GROW through it, and I am excitedly embracing every opportunity with gusto!

Besides, how can I feel anything less than empowered when I have people like you in my life? Thank you for being here with me each week, for reading my emails and for standing by in the wings waiting for your part in the play—you're going to all be STARS in the spotlight in your own ways. Your presence gives me strength when I am feeling a little less than. The emotions ebb and flow, but my commitment to you and **Uniquely U.** is unwavering.

As I told myself a long time ago, "*someday...I have faith!*"

And BTW—Mattie and I are living our 'Someday' and it is beyond anything I could have hoped for! Faith, willingness and fortitude were and continue to be the magic ingredients.

Make this week amazing!!!

Uniquely Yours,
Angela DiMarco, *Founder/CEO*

Find Uniquely U. Weekly Update #19

Sent: Thurs, May 27, 2021, at 12:25 PM

"Sorry I'm late. I got caught up at home being happy." [1]

Hello friends!

Going to keep this week's general update short and sweet because I'm about to reach out to all the U-Instructors with important information. If you do not receive a separate email but would like to be invited to the party, please reply back to this with the request to add your email to U-Instructor communications.

As far as biz development is going...I'm like 90% done with the Business Plan, and it is really impressive (if I don't say so myself! hehe!) I feel confident speaking so highly of my efforts because, well, when it did it become taboo to give ourselves a good old pat on the back? I mean, if we are uncomfortable recognizing our own achievements, then we tend to look outward for someone else to do it. And then when they don't, we feel frustration and shame for even desiring that atta boy/girl/person!

Not *this* girl! I have worked too hard on my self-worth to put the onus on someone else to recognize it. I'm proud of just about everything I do and achieve, even if it is as small as asking a friend for some help to work through a problem instead of muscling through it on my own (Dana, check is in the mail–LOL!!)

What personal achievements are YOU proud of? I'll ask this in our Facebook group. I would really love for you to fill the comments with shameless, fearless self-bragging!

Uniquely Yours,
Angela DiMarco, *Founder/CEO*

1. *These genius New Yorker cartoons are worth a quick scroll:* https://www.newyorker.com/culture/2018-in-review/instagrams-favorite-new-yorker-cartoons-of-2018

Uniquely U. Update #19

Sent: Tues, June 1, 2021, at 11:15 PM

Saturday May 29, 2021, 10:00am,
pouring rain on Long Island, NY.

Angela: *"Airshow was cancelled. I am so bummed.*
What else could we do today?"

Dave: *"Ha, we should just hop on a plane and go somewhere."*

Angela: (cross-checking non-stop flights out of MacArthur
airport)...*"Huh, want to go to Orlando at 2:30 today?"*

Dave: *"Sure, but where would we stay?"*

Angela: (checking Marriott Bonvoy site for ideas)...
"How about the Sheraton Vistana? It has a fun pirate ship
pool for Christian."

Dave: *"Okay, here's my credit card. You book the tickets, I'll start*
packing. What time do we have to leave for the airport?
12:30? Got it!"

(11:45am) Mattie: *"I decided I want to come, is it too late?"*

Angela: (booking Mattie's seats on the flights) *"Okay, you have 20 min to shower and pack!"*

Sometimes you just have to be spontaneous, right? #YOLO!

In the Facebook group, I asked members to share stories of their spontaneity. Some good ones there!! Please share yours if you haven't done so already.

I love traveling, especially with my family. The kids were amazing. Christian slept almost the whole flight back. Everything was just chaotically perfect, and I am feeling relaxed and blessed. Tomorrow is another day to get work done, but this past weekend was a time to remember.

I'd like to give a shout out to the man who made this happen—Dave, you are the best husband and father! Thank you for making these magical memories even possible!

That's all I've got for this week. Head is still in the clouds, and my ears are still unpopped. Until next week, stay crazy, my friends!!!

Uniquely Yours,
Angela DiMarco, *Founder/CEO*

Uniquely U. Update #20/21

Sent: Tues, June 8, 2021, at 3:33 PM

Playing on FindURadio today:

All Kinds of Time, by Fountains of Wayne

from their album "Welcome Interstate Managers."

Good day, Sunshines!

So, I just realized that I had sent out two #19 updates. It's so funny because I was waiting to make some big deal about having sent out 20 weeks of updates, and it just went under the radar! This little oversight has me pondering on the relevance of time...

When it comes to my kids and family, time moves way too quickly. With the day job, it moves way too slowly (I become Fred Flintstone when the 4:30pm whistle blows!) But with this business, time just isn't moving the way it usually does. Not too fast. Not too slow. I'm completely at peace and content with how things are going. Of course, I am EXCITED to do the next thing on my tasks list. I can't WAIT to tell you all that we are fully funded. I am EAGER to get the platform up and running for all of you. But I am also patient and trusting the process. This is very new for me and oddly very comfortable (did someone spike my brownies or something??? Who am I?!)

But really...I can see the big picture here...the whole field. I know my first-string teammates are going to crush it. I feel so confident playing this game, so made for this, so ready for whatever comes...Like the band Fountains of Wayne sing in the song, I feel like I've got "all kinds of time..."

"So, Ang, what's the play?" Huddle up and I'll tell you...

The business plan is still nearing completion, but the next project at hand is creating a promo video of sorts to help investors, first wave students, and U-Instructors understand what this is all about. Our awesome video editor is standing by waiting for footage to weave into a beautiful story. We have some amazing footage from the Brand DNA Workshop from a few months ago, and I am figuring out how I will find the courage and location to shoot myself telling the story of how this all came to be and what Uniquely U. is all about.

Be featured in the Uniquely U. video!

It is important that investors know *who and why me*, but it is equally, if not more so, important that they understand *who and why U!* If you feel inclined, shoot a little video on your phone or computer of yourself sharing your *Why U* using the lead-in, "I'm excited for Uniquely U. because..." or if you've known me for a long time and not really sure why Uniquely U, use the lead-in "Why (do I trust/invest/believe in) Angela? ..."

Email your video to me and please include your physical address so I can send you a little thank you prezzie in the mail!

Do you have any recommendations for:
- Corporate Lawyer/Law Firm
- Assistant well-versed using LinkedIn
- Contacts at the Gaia Network

Well, lovelies, that's all I have for this week's update. Please feel free to share these emails or the website FindUniquelyU.com to anyone in your life who will benefit from joining this community.

As always, I am so grateful for you!

I hope your whole week is Yabba-Dabba-Do-rific!

Uniquely Yours,

Angela DiMarco, *Founder/CEO*

Uniquely U. Update #22

Sent: Fri, June 18, 2021, at 4:05 PM

Hello Friends!

I would like to thank and welcome all of you who joined the list to receive these updates! Just to give a little refresher on what this whole thing is really about, here is an excerpt from the Master Business Plan. Please contact me with any questions you may have.

At the most fundamental level, **Uniquely U.** is a web-based, "extra education" platform and social network. There are four core pillars of our platform that set us apart:

1. **Students** (anyone ages 15–99, give or take a few years, with access to the Internet)
2. **U-Instructors** (vetted folks who feel called to teach. The only requirements are a passion for and knowledge of their offering)
3. **U-Social Network** (designed as if LinkedIn and Facebook had a baby)

4. **Hello! Pages / U-Campus Store** (public listings for businesses, content creators, craftspeople, products, etc.)

In and of themselves, these four pillars are not groundbreaking concepts. Comparatively, such as a wine producer perfects the com-bination of grapes, soil, sun and barrel to craft a corked symphony, **Uniquely U.** is the perfect combination of learning, teaching, networking, self-promoting, connecting, growing and even enlightening.

This has been a super productive week for Uniquely U. progress!

I've retained a fantastic attorney (Timothy Wan, Esq.) who is already providing sound counsel. Originally, I created an S-Corporation for the business, but my attorney explained that an LLC is much easier for our business model. I don't know about you, but I am not one to hem and haw over every little decision, especially when I seek advice from people who are experienced in matters that I am not and whom I respect. Within minutes of getting off our zoom call, I created a new entity called **The Uniquely U. Group LLC** (that should make you happy, Raina! Rolls off the tongue a bit better, right?) Just sharing this for the folks who have been following my adventures of entrepreneurship because some of our branding is going to change. For now, the URL, **FindUniquelyU.com**, will remain the same.

Speaking of adventures, not every experience is roses and candy. Last week, I received a really unprofessional email from a friend of a friend who is an investor. In between the contempt and insults were some sound pieces of advice that I vetted with people I trust to be true. Yes, it ruffled my feathers a bit (I mean, who wants to be insulted for just being me?), but I worked through my own issues of self-worthiness and acceptance with a little help from my friends and was able to take the good and shake my head with the bad. I'm sure that will not be the last of that lesson I need to learn, but hopefully it will sting less each time.

I also created some fun swag for those of you who are sending me a little video snippet for the promo video! If you haven't sent it yet, the deadline is by next weekend, June 26th. Message me for details if you are interested in being featured in the video.

Now onto the most important message this week:

" 'Father' is the noblest title a man can be given. It is more than a biological role. It signifies a patriarch, a leader, an exemplar, a confidant, a teacher, a hero, a friend."

~ Robert L. Backman

Thank you to all the men in our lives who have been blessed with the name 'Dad' or 'Grandpa', especially to my husband Dave. You are our rock, our greatest supporter, our most trusted provider. You give us the freedom to fly! Happy Father's Day—we love you!

Have a fantastic week, my friends!

Uniquely Yours,
Angela DiMarco, *Founder/CEO*

Uniquely U. Update #23

Sent: Fri, June 25, 2021, at 11:47 PM

> "Your work is to discover your world and
> then with all your heart give yourself to it."
> ~ Gautama Buddha

Happy Friday night, Friends!

Dave and I have started hunting for our new home this week and it has taken up a lot of my already limited brain space. As if working a full-time job, starting a new business, expanding my awareness and taking care of a toddler and teenager weren't enough! Just add 'buying a house in an insane seller's market' to my psych ward admin papers. Ha...I kid. I've got this! Sort of...

Want to know my secret to keeping my shit together and keeping this smile on my face and in my heart? It's simple, really. At the first sign of distress or emotional uncomfortability, I acknowledge the feeling and look inward. If the source of my discomfort is not easily apparent, I simply ask for help. That's it! That's the secret! Groundbreaking, right?

The fact is that the initial act of just reaching out to a friend or a colleague starts to change the trajectory of the situation. Then, when I get to talk to them, the solution becomes clearer. Usually by the time I hang up the phone, I am in a better, lighter mood, and I feel like I have actionable steps that I can take that will lead me towards contentment.

I am so grateful to have all different types of people to help me in moments like these, and it is ALL thanks to Uniquely U.! From New Zealand and Ireland to Toronto and all over the U.S., there are at *least* 20 of you that I know I can call right now and ask for help sorting things out in my life. What you do for me, you do so freely with others in your lives. I am so excited for this platform to be built so your light can shine like the beacons you are, sparking lights within new friends all over the world.

If anyone is struggling or just needs to talk, reach out to me. If I can't help, I can connect you with someone in our community who would be more than happy to!

Uniquely U. is now a proud member of COMMON!

Who is COMMON, you ask? Oh, just this amazing community of social businesses around the world helping each other come alive and thrive! I have already made some fantastic connections and new friends, and I've received expert guidance on next steps for our business growth. This support unequivocally bolsters my confidence.

Uniquely U. is entering our fundraising stage!

Woohoo! But wait, don't pop the sparkling grape juice yet. While we are armed and ready with our businessy information, there is still an unknown road ahead of us. But I have my hiking boots on, my canteen is full and my heart is PUMPED! Oh, and hey, our lawyer is working on our very first partner agreement, which will be presented in two weeks! (eek!) Once the check is in hand, I will introduce you to our newest partner. It's super exciting and I'm beyond grateful for this person's unwavering trust in me.

To put things in perspective, back in November, Uniquely U. was a concept scribbled in my notebook. I read it to Dana, and she saw the immediate, necessary value this would provide to the world and has since continued to be my source of encouragement. In January, I started reaching out and talking to just about anyone who would take a meeting (Norah, you introduced me to Peter and Harvey, founders of a new networking platform—you guys were my launching pad!) Then my pals from Victor Oddo's group and George J. jumped aboard, and well—yadda, yadda, yadda—here we are seven months later looking to raise 400k to build this extraordinary business. It's kinda blowing my mind right now how REAL this is getting!

As Buddha suggested in the quote above, I have discovered my world, and I am giving my whole heart to it. The rewards? I couldn't have imagined the awesomeness of my life right now, and we've only just begun...

Thanks for reading. If you need someone to talk to, please reach out to me. We are all in this together. Have a magical week!

Uniquely Yours,

Angela DiMarco, *Founder/CEO*

Uniquely U. Update #24

Sent: Sat, July 3, 2021, at 10:43 AM

> "First, think.
>
> Second, dream.
>
> Third, believe.
>
> And finally, dare."
>
> ~ Walt Disney

Hello Friends,

What if we could ask Walt Disney for some elaborated words of wisdom? Perhaps he would remind us that we all have our own gifts, our own ways of sharing and spreading our light.

He might tell us to keep forward motion and positive focus on what we are doing, working toward our passion with hope, love, joy, and compassion with the shared goal of a better tomorrow.

In honor of sharing and celebrating gifts, each month, I'll be introducing different members of our extraordinary community to you.

I invite you to engage with them and get to know them. Each person is unique and authentic and amazing in their own ways...

Uniquely U. Member Spotlight

Michelle Golinski

What courses are you planning to offer on Uniquely U.? I would like to offer courses or workshops that empower people to find answers and/or connect with Spirit for themselves. Everyone has the ability to heal themselves and connect with Spirit/God/Universe/Source—whatever they choose to call it. They often just don't realize it on a conscious level. I would like what-ever I do to be very interactive.

As a student, what types of courses will you be looking to sign up for? I don't believe I'll know the answer to this until I read the description of each offered course. I lean towards the esoteric/metaphysical, but I'm also intrigued by creative and practical offerings as well. I never know what will spark my interest.

What is something you would like the Uniquely U. community to know about you? I would like people to know that I am not just the "Spiritual" person. I have degrees in accounting and English literature and have also done all but my student teaching for my certification in middle school and high school education. My work experience includes an extensive background with real estate-based law firms as a paralegal, title examiner and office manager. Unfortunately, when people only know you as doing spiritual, metaphysical, or energy work, they tend to label you as flighty, airy-fairy, or woo-woo! But I am educated and have worked in corporate/professional jobs for many of my adult years.

What advice do you have for your 15-year-old self? I would tell my younger self that not fitting in is a gift to be treasured. Being different and unique is a positive—embrace it. Never be afraid or ashamed of your emotions. There is a reason you notice things and feel things on a seemingly exaggerated level. Someday all of this will be obvious and will serve you well—listen to your instincts and your gut. Do not discount your own intuition for the advice of others. Follow your own path—dismiss the "shoulds." Be true to your Self and your own desires. The ultimate goal is to connect with Christ/God Consciousness—the earlier you realize this, the better life will be. Don't let religion chase you away or make you turn your back on your connection with God/Christ/Source/Universe/Spirit! And yes...I do use all those names interchangeably.

ANNOUNCEMENT

Uniquely U. Web Development Partner Scopic Software

After many meetings, intense evaluation and deep considera-tion, I am pleased to announce that we will be partnering with ScopicSoftware.com to bring our platform to life! This global team has the experience we need and the flexibility to adapt our platform based on your input and requests.

My family and I are heading down to Florida to visit Walt's magical world for a week. I will not be bringing my laptop or working on ANYTHING but being fully present with my favorite people. My brain needs some much-needed R&R (Rest and Repair, as Dana likes to say!) I will not be sending an update out next week, but the following, I hope to have a HUGE announce-ment for you all! It's getting real, my friends! Can you feel it?

Be well. And enjoy the 4th of July fireworks if you are in the states!

Uniquely Yours,

Angela DiMarco, *Founder/CEO*

Uniquely U. Update #25

Sent: Wed, July 14, 2021, at 3:29 PM

Hello Friends!

This week, I have a HUGE ANNOUNCEMENT!!!

Dana Sardano Sgambellone, with the support of her dashing husband Rob, has signed on to be our first Uniquely U. business partner! Not only has Dana contributed a SIGNIFICANT investment to our start-up capital goals, her emotional investment backed by her unwavering belief in the need for this platform to exist is going to catapult us into the next level!

For those of you who don't know our story, back in 1992, Dana was my Sigma Delta Tau pledge mom at the University of South Florida. Everyone called me 'Little Dana'—I was in awe of her then as much as I am today. We lost touch after college, but thanks to good old social media, we reconnected about five years ago as 'Facebook friends' with the occasional message or comment here or there.

We were led to really reconnect back in October-ish last year (2020) and have since had a magical friendship. I am so impressed with what Dana has built in her life. She's not only a beautiful artist and creator, but she's also a brilliant author, savvy business owner and insightful intuitive. And above all, Dana is as loyal and as trustworthy as they come.

To be clear, this partnership is not just about two friends helping each other out. This is so much bigger. This is about two smart entrepreneurs seizing an opportunity to be catalysts in shifting paradigms and helping humanity level up. My only hope is to bring on a select few additional partners who can bring a quarter of what Dana brings to the table.

So, my friends, we are well on our way now to making this idea a reality! We are a third of the way to raising the capital we need to put this project into motion! Boo-freakin-ya!

Prior to meeting up with Dana and Rob, we had a fantastic Disney/Palm Beach vacation. I left my laptop home, and it was liberating to give the old noggin a much needed break. Christian was amazing given that we hit four parks in two days while contending with Hurricane Elsa (which wasn't really even that bad—she hit NY much worse!) Everything just seemed to work out perfectly the whole time we were there. No stress. Lots of good food and laughs! I love traveling, especially with this crazy awesome crew! The fireworks at Epcot were Epic, especially since we watched from our dinner table at the Rose & Crown in England. So civilized!

There's magic in the air, friends! Can you feel it?

Breathe it in and relax because things are about to get bonkers!

Uniquely Yours,

Angela DiMarco, *Founder/CEO*

Uniquely U. Update #26

Sent: Wed, July 21, 2021, at 10:38 PM

"Do you see the way that tree bends?
Does it inspire?
Leaning out to catch the sun's rays
A lesson to be applied
Are you getting something out of this
all-encompassing trip?"

Lyrics from the song *Present Tense* by Pearl Jam

Good morning, afternoon or evening,

(depending on where you are in the world when you read this),

(which is pretty darn cool that we are spanning all time zones now!)

(... wow, taking a moment to absorb that!)

Okay, back to the present tense, which is currently 9:58pm EST here on Long Island, NY.

As I've mentioned, Dave and I are house hunting. It's a really interesting experience, as I am learning so much about myself.

I've learned that when I walk through a house and picture how our family would fit in it to not get emotionally attached. Otherwise, the disappointment is just too heavy. And I've learned that when I am disappointed but say "I'm Fine!", I'm not fine, and the disappointment comes out in other ways until I recognize it, accept it and move forward.

I've also realized that Dave and I are pretty much on the same page and provide a great balance for each other—he is grounded in reality, and I'm the visionary.

For example, today we saw a cute little house that just popped up on the market. We were greeted by this cute, young girl who broke down in tears because she and her newish husband were getting a divorce. She loved this home she now had to sell—I felt her pain.

I couldn't say this to her, but I was also excited for her! She is going to learn so much about herself through this painful experience (no pain, no gain, amiright?), and I just felt that something AMAZING is on her horizon. Through her tears and sadness, I could see the little flame sparking inside her, and once she gets through grieving this life she had planned, she is going to skyrocket into a new dimension of joy.

I so badly wanted to buy this house so that we could continue to love it FOR her, but then practical Dave pointed out all the things that didn't work for our family, which I was open to hearing and agreed with. He really is the creamy peanut butter to my strawberry jam.

Obviously, my pendulum has a wide swing. I don't know about you, but I can have ten things running through my brain at once, and it can get exhausting! Being in the present moment forces me to be more balanced, to prioritize all the tasks running through my mind and to focus on one thing at a time, even if that one thing is doing nothing for 10 min. and giving myself a reset.

Raising money for a company that I am starting up is really out of my comfort zone, so my tendency is to distract myself with safer tasks. But by being mindful and present, I gain clarity and confidence, and I jump on opportunities using my newly sharpened discernment tool. It's pretty empowering, I have to say!

Before I sign off for the night, would you mind helping me with something? I am questioning the placement of this 'Note from Our Founder' (below) in the business plan. I currently close with it, but I am wondering if this should be in the lead, like a preface to the business plan.

I am always asked, "Why this? Why now?"...

Up until 2008, I thought I had it all. I owned an apartment in Brooklyn, had a great job in NYC, a beautiful daughter and a healthy bank account and an excellent credit score. But the recession hit, and everything changed. I left an abusive husband and shortly after, I was laid off from my advertising job. Instead of finding another full-time job, I tried freelancing so I could have flexibility to care for my daughter but finding clients and getting paid were tough. After all the divorce fees and living in the city while unemployed as a single mom, I was close to 100k in debt. I remember counting change so I could buy my daughter a slice of pizza after school. After a near nervous breakdown in the spring of 2010, I became a member of an amazing program that changed my life. I knew deep down that I had to start healing from within in order to build the life that I dreamed of.

During that time, I could have really used a community like this— a place to learn how to nurture clients and how to market myself, a place that I could source work from and learn how to be a single mom while freelancing, a place to connect and learn from people who were once in my situation...it would have been helpful to have the support of a village, as I was very much alone and very much winging it.

It is looking back on this time in my life and hearing of people's experiences of reinventing themselves due to the pandemic that sparked the idea for this platform. No one should have to suffer to put food on the table. Not today. Not ever. **There is opportunity for anyone who reaches for it**—for the little dogs to get the big bones. All they need to do is find their true, unique skills and follow their hearts to do what they are passionate about. Success is the byproduct. I've seen it time and time again.

Since 2010, my life has changed immensely. I am grateful to have a supportive and nurturing partnership with my husband. My baby girl is now 16 years old and is an amazing big sister to our brilliant 3-year-old son. Now that my family and heart are whole, I want to give back to the global community, and hopefully make it so that no one has to ever dig up loose change to buy their kid a slice of pizza after school.

~ Angela DiMarco, Founder/CEO, Uniquely U.

Thanks for indulging me! It is presently 10:36pm, and I am off to have some Yogi tea and Schitt's Creek with the hubby before drifting off to sleep. Good night and Good morrow!

Uniquely Yours,

Angela DiMarco, *Founder/CEO*

Uniquely U. Update #27

Sent: Thurs, July 29, 2021, at 12:39 AM

"Your total mega-meltdown tantrum really helped me see your side of things."

Said no mom ever.

someecards
user card

(yawn...) Good Evening, Friends...

I can't believe a week has passed since I last wrote to you! Christian, my newly turned 3 year old, is getting over a little cold, so with him home from daycare and trying to work, this week has been a blur. Don't get me wrong, I LOVE having him home, especially when I can really MOM him up and care for him. But now that he feels better, he needs the attention of his wonderful teachers and friends to enrich that developing brain of his. I just can't do that and work at the same time or angst and chaos ensue (mostly in MY overloaded brain.)

I just want to share a pretty intense/interesting experience that we had earlier.

I have to build about six physical Uniquely U. presentations for potential investors, as my dear friend is waiting patiently for them (Friday—PROMISE!), so I dragged my exhausted, grumpy toddler to Staples to pick up some supplies. I promised him one item of his choosing if he helped me shop.

So firstly, because I was so distracted by Christian taking everything off the shelves saying, "What's this? I want it. And what's this? I want it! (and so on)," I misplaced my credit card that I was carrying (I hate purses much to my aunt's dismay!) So we had a fun game of hunting for that (I found it sandwiched between some divider tab packs I had decided against)...whew, okay. Handled that one with just a little touch of anxiety.

Christian picked out some Crayola paints and we made our way to the register, and that is when all hell broke loose. Now, my son has been gifted with a very...loud...voice and when he is pissed, he screeches at such a pitch that glass could break (someday this will serve him well, I am sure of it!) As I approach-ed the register, I realized that I took a box of the wrong size binders, so the manager helped me by going in the back to look for the right box. I knew where it was, but I was already rung up so she told me to wait there.

Christian fixated on some Sharpies and asked me very sweetly if he could have them because he knew the answer would be "no", and when I didn't give in and say yes to his adorable face, he proceeded to screech at the top of his lungs. I'm sure the next town over heard him. Everyone in line started giving me that look (mom's, you KNOW that look, right?) Of course, I didn't give in, so I just distracted him as best I could, soothe him (he *was* really tired), shot apologizing glances to the mom in line behind me, who kept asking the one girl up front if someone else could ring her up like now please.

For 15 minutes, we stood there while they hunted for my binders in the back. 15 MINUTES of Christian screeching "Permanent Markers!!! I WANT THEM!!!!!"—snot and tears running down his face for which I had no tissues, so I used my sweater to wipe him up. 15 Minutes of the line getting longer and the looks getting more frustrated. I wanted to give up and walk out, but I really needed these supplies tonight, so we waited. Finally, she came back up front and said she couldn't find them, so I paid for my other stuff and was about to walk out to spare everyone's ears, but I still needed those dang binders. So, I carried my 35 lb, sobbing, snotty son to the back of the store, picked up the heavy box of binders and walked back up front and waited at the back of the line to buy them, all the while he was just beside himself with grief for these home-wrecking markers!

I turned to a group of people who were witness to the whole thing and said, "If this isn't just the perfect picture of a mom entrepreneur, I don't know what is!" and they politely laughed because they had no idea what I was talking about (their energy didn't exactly exude an entrepreneur spirit.) As I locked my snotty, crying kid in his car seat and closed the door, I inhaled the evening summer air and regrouped.

I'm telling you this long story because that little phrase that came out of my mouth actually filled me with so much pride. Hell yes, I am doing whatever I need to do for my business in the small window of opportunity I find while handling the most monstrous of tantrums with grace and compassion! By the way, Christian cried all the way to his bath, and then acted like nothing freakin' happened! Toddlers!

On Another (Founder's) Note:

Thanks to your feedback and help with some edits, I've decided to put the Founder's Note on the website instead of just in the investor presentation. Now everyone can understand where this idea came from and why I am so passionate about building this platform. If you feel so inclined, please share with your network.

That's all I've got for this week. Thanks for letting me get that story out. I needed to process and release it. And now I must get some rest.

As my Grammy always used to say, "Sweet Dreams!"

Uniquely Yours,
Angela DiMarco, *Founder/CEO*

Uniquely U. Update #28

Sent: Wed, Aug 4, 2021, at 10:51 PM

"Home is a refuge not only from the world,
but a refuge from my worries, my troubles,
my concerns."

~ Maya Angelou

Happy Wednesday, Friends!

Dave and I have an accepted offer on a house! We found out yesterday. Man, was this a test to our strength and patience! Of course, nothing is final yet, but now that the offer has been accepted, and we feel we made a really great decision for our family, I feel like I can breathe and let this massive portion of my plate free up. What to do first??! (Yes, Michelle, Dana and Wendy, I will take the time to be still and quiet! Hahahah.)

I don't know if you know this about me, but from the time that my daughter was 5 until she was 12, her father had residential custody of her. Those of you that know me and even who lived through that chapter with me know that the situation with her father was not pretty. I used to carry great shame about this, especially in the beginning. But as the years passed, Mattie and I grew closer and closer, and I learned and grew in that great period of intense emotions. Today, I don't talk about it openly, strictly because of the implication it has on who I am and my character due to our social conditioning. But I am really, really proud of myself for walking through those years with my head held high. I did the work within, and I'm seriously in awe when I look back on what the year 2010 looked like compared to what my life looks like today in 2021. It's beyond miraculous!

What does my daughter have to do with buying our home? Well, thanks to good old Facebook look backs, it was on **August 3, 2017** that it became official that Mattie was coming to live with Dave and me, embarking on a new chapter that has been nothing short of the light-filled *yang* to the dark *ying* of the previous seven years. And it was yesterday, **August 3, 2021** that we found out about our new home! We are turning the page at the end of the most enlightening and most wonderful chapters of my life so far, and I just can't wait to find out what comes next!

NEW: Ask Angela Anything!

Are there any questions I can answer for you? I am always at your service. Simply reply to this email with your question or hit me up on Facebook.

This week, @SarahArtly asked: *I would love to know more about your preparation for meetings with potential investors. I have someone who has expressed interest in investing in me, so I would love some advice on how to be prepared for the meeting.*

First and foremost, how awesome and exciting! For me, having conversations with people who not only believe in my project but also have enough faith to throw a lot of skin in the game to help make it happen is beyond humbling (financial, emotional or otherwise!) It also taps into my self-worthiness issues, so it is a great opportunity to overcome them. The best thing for me feeling prepared is to, well, prepare almost to an OCD level. I have been working on laying the foundation for Uniquely U. since last November, really, getting as granular as I can about each piece of this puzzle—talking to you all and new people about it. I feel that this business runs through my very core, so I feel totally confident that I will slam a home run with any investor who pitches me curve balls. But I'll come back to you in a couple of weeks after I've had a few meetings to see if I can share anything I've learned. But the takeaway here is 1. know your 'product' (your content, your brand, your plan for getting traction, etc.), and 2. know your worth. I won't be cashing just any checks thrown at me (assuming they will be! manifesting!! LOL), but I will be vetting potential investors as much as they will be vetting me. After all, I am going to be giving away a good chunk of the pie to these people—they better be folks who align with my values, are raving fans of the platform and evangelists to help grow the business. Look at what this investor has to offer you, and *you* decide if it is a good fit. You are in the driver's seat. Please keep me posted! I'm so proud of you, and it is truly miraculous to watch you blossom!

@CharlieSinger asked: *If someone wants to teach how would they apply to teach a class? It's actually me. I think I know what I want to teach to help people with. I know I can talk to you but what about someone new who doesn't know the crew?*

Thanks for this question, Charlie! This is so timely because I was going to speak to our resident and future U-Instructors in this very email! So, the first step is to go to the U-Instructor section on FindUniquelyU.com and watch my little video where I talk about being a U-Instructor. Then, fill out the form on that page and submit your high-level ideas for your course/s. This will put you on the U-Instructor email communications, which I am going to start gearing back up soon because we have to start REALLY preparing the courses—isn't that exciting!!??! I can't wait to see what your course is going to be!

ATTENTION! All Interested U-Instructors

Please stay tuned for more details in the coming week or so. We are going to start pulling your course info from the form you filled out a while ago. If you haven't done so, please go to FindUniquelyU.com and provide as much information on the application as you can. Don't worry, we are going to help you organize your courses with checklists, templates and training materials (all of which will be in development as time allows).

Investor Presentations

Speaking of presentations, I've made eight books for existing and potential investors. Six more have been 'ordered' by my colleague who is helping to get the word out on joining in on this exciting and potentially highly lucrative opportunity.

If you know of anyone who might be interested, please reach out to me and I can send you digital or even a hard copy of this deck to them. If a contact of yours becomes an investor, I will throw in a nice finder's fee for your connection!

Well friends, if you've made it this far, thank you for sticking with me through this week's newsletter! No tantrums this week. Just one happy, (very close to being a) homeowner! Life is beautiful and it unfolds in perfect timing.

> "You'll see it when you believe it."
> ~ Dr. Wayne W. Dyer

Uniquely Yours,
Angela DiMarco, *Founder/CEO*

Uniquely U. Update #29

Sent: Thurs, Aug 12, 2021, at 10:37 PM

"Make the best of it and
find gratitude in every little moment.
There is *always* a reason to smile."

~ My text to my 16-year-old who was recently a little anxious.

I hope this email finds you well and happy, friends!

I realize that it might seem weird that I am quoting myself above, but sometimes things come out of my mouth, and I look around thinking, "who just said that nugget?" Does that happen to you, too? I was attempting to console my anxious daughter, and in doing so, I soothed my own feelings of trepidation over our house. Which, by the way, we are in the contract stage! With each new stage, there is immediate relief followed quickly by lingering anxiety over clearing the next hurdle. I had an amazing dream the other night about unpacking in our new home and opening doors that revealed things like extra storage space that I hadn't known was there (room for new memories!), a daycare, a retail gym-like-place and a business center. I interpreted that as meaning that this home will be the portal or gateway to the next phase of Uniquely U.!

So what's happening in the adventures of a "Mompreneur"?
(Thank you again, Michelle, for my favorite title ever!)

- 14 **Invest in U.** presentation books are in the hands of people who know people. I do believe that the investors will find us soon and we will be well on our way to building this thing. I've come across a few naysayers and know-betterers along the way. That can eat me up a bit, but with a little help from my friends and some perspective, I can take what I need from the situation, which is always something I learn about myself based on my reactions to it. And because of that, I am certainly not the same woman I was six months ago. How freaking cool is that? Total unexpected byproduct of starting up a new business!

- I've received the first Uniquely U. promo video edit from Take Two Productions and it's amazing! We're making some tweaks, so it should be ready in the coming weeks. I can't wait to share it with you all. It's pretty exciting! :)

- My Soul Bro Charlie Singer has graciously volunteered to help me start organizing all the courseware we have so far. For those of you who have filled out the form, be on the lookout in the coming weeks for an email from Charlie. He's going to check in with you, see if you are still on board to become a U-Instructor and answer any questions you may have. If you haven't signed up and are interested in teaching a course, please fill out the form, even if it is high level information so you can be a part of the initial U-Instructor roster.

- I can't believe that this update is #29. Some of you have been reading my ramblings for 29 weeks! I can't express how thankful I am for your support and your time to read my emails, shoot me back notes, engage in the Facebook group, etc. You are the foundation of this platform, and I am so excited to bring this all to life for all of you!

Once we are fully funded, it is going to be go-time, BIG time, so I am enjoying this calm before the storm, embracing the simplicity and easy routine of my days, and I'm focusing on the next hurdle to get us to home sweet home. And by storm, I don't know if you agree, but there is nothing better than a good thunderstorm when I'm inside cozied up by an open window listening to the torrential rain with a hot coffee in hand. I'm so excited for the Uniquely U. storm to blow in with all the unanticipated surprises!!

Until next week, my friends!

I hope you find a reason to smile in all of your moments.

Uniquely Yours,

Angela DiMarco, *Founder/CEO*

Uniquely U. Update #30

Sent: Wed, Aug 18, 2021, at 10:55 AM

Hello, Sunshines of My Life!

This month's U. Member Spotlight features Dana Sardano. Particularly for those of you who don't know this amazing woman.

Uniquely U. Member Spotlight

Dana Sardano

From Day 1, you have been an unconditionally supportive friend as I've developed the concept of this platform. But friendship alone is not what drove you to become my first (and most special!) investment partner. Why did you decide to invest in Uniquely U.? For me, investing in Uniquely U. was a no brainer. Although Uniquely is a ground breaking platform that will be no doubt far reaching and influential and truly bring forth a sense of personal autonomy as well as sense of community for the masses, my investment is in its founder. Angela, what you have created over the last six months or so, with your vision, resolve, and attention to detail, is nothing short of astounding. I'd hitch my cart to this pony any day of the week!

What is your offering to the world? Presently, I think my offering is my willingness to do the work, the real hands-on difficult work towards self-discovery and personal empowerment, which ultimately leads to peace and freedom and my openness with sharing it with the world—the good, the bad, and the ugly.

What is something you are struggling with at the moment? (I chuckle) The ugly part of that previous answer.

What do you do that brings you the most joy? Oh my God! So many things—first and foremost, conversations with my husband and children at the dinner table. If one of us isn't spitting out our drink in laughter at the table, then our job as parents has not been done!

What is something you are most proud of? I've been involved in creating some really cool stuff recently, but of what I'm most proud is the life I have created for myself and my family. Breaking the cycle of toxicity in the home and creating a safe and loving environment for my children where they can grow and thrive truly brings me the most pride.

What is something you would like the Uniquely U. community to know about you? Barry Manilow is my favorite musical artist, but if you ask me in mixed company, I will tell you The Doors. Got it?!

What is one of your favorite quotes?
"That's what she said." ~Michael Scott, The Office

Also,

"In Essence, we all have the magic within us. We all are born with love, truth, intuition, and connectedness, but when our foundation becomes cracked through the trauma of our experiences, our magic becomes buried in the rubble. Once we understand this and repair, restructure, and in some cases, rebuild our foundation, we reveal a whole new layer of ourselves, and life truly begins to become magical." ~Dana Sardano, *Ten Recommandments for Personal Empowerment*

(I know that one was me, but when I wrote it, I thought it was quite brilliant!

What advice do you have for your 12 yr. old self? You are as intelligent and beautiful and creative as you think you are, and you don't have to force anything or prove anything to anybody, ever. Just ignore your critics and keep honoring who you know you are and the opportunities to love and to learn and to grow will come to you on a silver platter. Life is to be enjoyed. Just enjoy it and learn from the rest. Most importantly, you are loved.

In retrospect...

Now that we are on Update #30, I thought it would be a useful exercise for me to look back through all these Uniquely U. updates and see how this platform and myself have evolved. I'll be posting them in the Facebook group and attaching them to these newsletters should you wish to join the journey from the very beginning. The first update was to the first of you who jumped on the train and THEN asked where we were heading— you guys are the foundation that gave me strength.

"This little light of mine, I'm gonna let it shine."

How have you been feeling lately? Are you experiencing frequent headaches, body aches and pains, a cold that won't go away? Are you feeling depressed or more anxious than usual? You are not alone. There is a massive, global upheaval happening all around us, and it's tricky to not to get sucked into the weight of it all and despair for our future. But what that's really doing is trying to distract us from our own personal growth and expansion. A lot of us are going through some crazy stuff right now, so don't despair! There are some very simple things you can do to strengthen your resilience and nurture your wellbeing.

Turn off the news. Seriously. Take a breath and focus on the four walls around you. No media outlet is trustworthy—you're going to tune into the one who tells you what you want to hear, not necessarily what is the truth. The news simply sucks you down into the darkness and keeps you there by instilling fear at every turn. Take a break from the news like you would from sugar or carbs and watch your physical symptoms lighten. My life has become enormously more wonderful because I literally will only peek my head around the corner to hear the weather when Dave is watching News12, which is also never quite accurate, which I find amusing.

Focus inward. This is your time to really look at your life today and assess all that is making you feel joyful and all that's bringing you down. If something makes you happy, then do more of it. If something is bringing you down, spend some time focusing on it. What about it is making you not feel good? Are there relationships with friends or family that are uncomfortable or detrimental to your happiness? If so, are they repairable or is it time to cut the ties that bind you? I've had to make really hard choices to remove toxic people from my life over the years, and while it's super icky at the time, my peace and happiness on the other side are my reward. You do not need to cause World War

III to make the changes, you can simply make the decision that this person or situation is no good for you and then watch the universe conspire to create opportunities that remove it/them for you. It sounds like magic because it is!

Quiet your thoughts. Meditating doesn't necessarily mean sitting in a yoga position, chanting *OOHMMMMM* and listening to 'high vibe music' (which is what I always believed and struggled with). When you are doing chores, walking across a parking lot, taking a shower, exercising, etc., simply focus on what you are doing at the moment. If your mind wanders to your long to-do list and conversation replays, gently let that go and bring your thoughts back to your breath or the sun on your face or the birds chirping. This is the toughest one for me, as my mind has 42 stations playing at the same time. But when I DO do this, I realize how exhausting all this thinking really is, and I gain much needed peace of mind.

Listen to your gut. YOU know YOU best. Think about situations in the past where you followed your instincts and circumvented something that would have been an unpleasant experience. Whether you get a gut feeling or receive a random thought or see something that inspires an action, learn to follow these breadcrumbs, and trust your instincts.

If you are reading my newsletters, then chances are you are among MANY of us who are experiencing what the spiritual community calls 'ascension symptoms' and they are *no joke*—but they are *so worth it!* We can all survive the global turmoil if we do the inner work to shed the weight of our past experiences. This will raise our own vibration and thus affect those around us that we love, shedding light on all the darkness inside and out. It's a sensational phenomenon to witness! In order to nurture a more peaceful, more loving society, your only job is to do you, Boo!

Uniquely U. is built on these very concepts. By spending time with people who lift you up and by exploring your true heart's desires, we will create a community of happy, joyful, vivacious people traveling arm-in-arm on our journey of self-discovery and enlightenment.

Be fearless, for there is *nothing* to fear.
We've got your back!

Uniquely Yours,
Angela DiMarco, *Founder/CEO*

Uniquely U. Update #31

> "Feel like a question is forming
> And the answer's far
> I will be what I could be
> Once I get out of this town
> For the lights of this city
> They have lost all feeling
> Gonna leave 'em all behind me
> 'Cause this time I'm gone"
>
> Lyrics from the song *Gone* by Pearl Jam

Hello Dear Friends,

It's been a pensive, unique time for many of us, hasn't it? I for one have been an emotional hermit crab these past couple of weeks. I haven't been too active on social media, and I've only connected with a few friends here and there. I don't know...I suppose there is a sense that this time in my life is all about to change, so I am just letting the gratitude steep, integrating all I am learning and resting before riding the next wave of awesomeness. I sincerely hope that you are all resting too because you'll be a huge part of Uniquely U.!

Retrospectively, this Pearl Jam song "Gone" was released back in 2006 just after Mattie was born. Her entering this world was the start of my awakening to who I truly was. Up until her birth,

I was an aimless tornado that created a path of destruction for anyone who got caught in the frenzy of it all, but mostly for myself. So, when this song came out, I had started really looking around me and moving on from or going towards all that led to me becoming my true self, from the job and the marriage to the friends and the passions (like playing music). This song was an anthem of that time in my life.

Of course, I've listened to this song thousands of times since 2006, but this past weekend, I 'heard' it again—but now, I relate to leaving my old identity behind as I drive along the high road towards new adventures. There is an obvious distancing happening from who I was even just a few months ago, and instead of the sadness, pain, and regret of yesteryear, I feel content, proud, and accomplished.

The biggest burden I've carried with me since childhood has been my lack of self-worth, which is not the best trait an entrepreneur can have. To be totally honest, it has been a struggle. But I feel the distance growing wider and wider between that insecure girl I once was and this worthy, empowered woman that I am becoming.

And there are incredible byproducts from building this confidence, like patience! After building a business plan and investor presentations and a website and a Facebook group and a community of amazing like-minded people, the fact that I am uncharacteristically sitting back and resting and putting the next step 100% in the hands of the universe is nothing short of a miracle. Yet here I sit and nary a drop of sweat on my brow. *Who AM I?* Okay, maybe there's a little excited anticipation, but what I have planned for you guys is really something to be excited about!

Regarding the place where we will finally plant our roots, the house passed inspection with flying colors, and now we await the appraisal which is scheduled for this coming Friday. Hoping we close by Update #35.

The rest of our Uniquely U. funding is coming because I am almost ready for it. The timing is always perfect (trust—another awesome byproduct!)

Over these past few months, I haven't had much to report on the business side of things, so thank you for indulging me by reading my musings. My hope is for those of you who don't know me to get to know me so that when we are in the trenches together in the coming months, you'll feel connected and appreciated.

I LOVE hearing from you! Reply to this email and tell me how you are doing and what you are looking forward to in the coming weeks. If we haven't really chatted yet, please tell me a little bit about yourself, like what makes your heart sing.

While I may be "Gone" from my old life and old self, WE are...

"Movin' right along
in search of good times and good news,
With good friends you can't lose,
This could become a habit!

Movin' right along.
Footloose and fancy-free.
Getting there is half the fun;
come share it with me."

Lyrics from the song *Moving Right Along* by Jim Henson's The Muppets

Uniquely Yours,

Angela DiMarco, *Founder/CEO*

Uniquely U. Update #32

Sent: Wed, Sept 1, 2021, at 9:48 AM

Welcome to September!

I just love the fall in New York. First day of school for the kids. Watching the leaves change colors. Crisp afternoons. Apple picking under cobalt blue skies. Sweater weather! I enjoy all the seasons for different reasons, but the fall and I have had a lifetime love affair. Most noteworthy things happen for me in the fall because my love of the season attracts the like. So, in my core, I just know that the Uniquely U. Express is pulling into the station any day now!

I am excited to present to you this video introducing Uniquely U. Shout out to the oh-so-talented company Take Two Productions for helping to tell our story (highly recommended!) To watch the video go to: youtu.be/5gRATHp_8OY

The finalization of this video means that it is TIME TO GET TO WORK! I was chatting with a potential investment partner and future U-Instructor yesterday and my heart was just bursting with excitement because I was reminded of the enormous potential **Uniquely U.** has for so many people. This platform is being created so ANYONE can teach ANYTHING they are passionate about and make some *good money* doing so.

Attention U-Instructors! Workshop course applications **due September 15th**.

Now is the time to start getting your courses sent over to me. There will be a limited offering in the beginning so as to not overwhelm inaugural members. If you have already submitted course ideas via the form on the website, then you are set. If you wrote to me with some ideas for courses but haven't filled out the form, please do so ASAP. In a couple of weeks, we will begin working with you to shape your workshops.

Video content ideas **due September 30th**.

Building our video library is going to be integral to not only keeping our members engaged on the platform but also to help promote U-Instructors and your workshops. Many of you have had some amazing video content ideas that I would really love to see come to fruition! Please fill out the form on the website with your ideas. Towards the end of the month, we will be reaching out with some structural and technical suggestions to help guide your content creation.

To give you an idea of the WIDE range of just some of the offerings we already have on the table, check out some of these workshop ideas being tossed around: The sky is the limit!

- *A publishing workshop going through in-depth, writing and editing, publishing (looking at self-publishing and traditional publishing), and book marketing.*
- *Advocacy course helping parents of children w/ disabilities.*
- *Podcasting and Authenticity*
- *Developing your psychic and mediumistic abilities.*
- *Vedic Astrology for Beginners*
- *Cover Letter and CV Writing / Acing That Interview*
- *Learn Classical Indian Music (Beginners)*
- *Basic home remodeling skills, covering basic common fixes, knowledge of what tools to have.*
- *Cold climate geodome greenhouses building.*
- *Journey into telepathy and the telepathic chakras.*
- *Communicate with your higher self, your guides, your intuition and your subconscious mind.*

So, start stretching. Oil up that glove. Get in the zone. It's almost game time!

Uniquely Yours,
Angela DiMarco, Founder/CEO

Uniquely U. Update #33

> "Gotta keep those
> lovin'good vibrations
> a-happenin'"

Lyrics from the song *Good Vibrations* by The Beach Boys

So, how are y'all doing?

The world outside is getting a little messy, a little more intense. The best way to combat it is to keep up those good vibrations!

Thank you to so many of you who offered your condolences last week. Dave and I read each one and were just so appreciative of your genuine and heartfelt thoughts. Uncle Edward was laid to rest yesterday in Veneta, OR and Dave and his mom are on their way home.

U-Instructors and Ownership of Content

A friend who has been with this endeavor since its inception brought up something that I didn't realize needed clarification. I have so many details in my head about this platform, and I don't want to inundate you with the minutia, but this is a big one that you all should know.

All U-Instructors are the **sole owner** of whatever content they teach. Uniquely U. is simply a platform to be utilized with a built-in audience and marketing support. Yes, we will help shape content and we will train and nurture those who want to teach but don't have experience, but what they bring to the table is their expertise and theirs alone. We hold no proprietary ownership over anything but how the platform is run. Think of us more like a combination of Facebook + Zoom + Home Advisor.

The only request is to not offer the same live workshop type course at a cheaper cost outside of Uniquely U. *while you are teaching it* so there are no competitive vibes. But self-promotion of your offerings outside of Uniquely U. are totally encourage-ed—that is our sweet, unique offering!

The library of videos-on-demand will be revenue-generators for the content-creators. They are available at no extra cost for the members, but the content-owners will be paid royalties at certain view benchmarks. We will simply add our branding to the front of the video with the title and end it with a link to the creator's Hello! Page listing, which will be their business website or social channels. Videos will be created by the U-Instructors and uploaded to our platform, at which time we will vet the content to make sure all is appropriate and technically viable.

Uniquely U. is a safe place for your content, your brand and your business. We are here for those who want to earn a little extra cash and grow their brand visibility, not to consume and own all that people have to offer. All one has to do is create a niche course around something they are passionate about, and we will make sure they are nurtured and supported. The whole idea is to help everyone expand, not just students, but U-Instructors too, in their own personal endeavors.

That being said, hopefully that opens the door for more of you to feel confident to submit the form outlining your ideas for videos or live workshops. **I am extending the deadline to submit for the first-string A-Team of U-Instructors to SEPTEMBER 30th** —hope to see some new entries! Hit me up if you have any questions.

I'm sorry.
Please forgive me.
Thank you.
I love you.
~ Ho'oponopono Healing Prayer

Uniquely Yours,
Angela DiMarco, *Founder/CEO*

Uniquely U. Update #34

Sent: Wed, Sept 22, 2021, at 4:39 PM

Happy Wednesday, Friend.

This month's U. Member Spotlight features my friend and colleague George Jacobs. Click below to read the interview.

\---------------------

Uniquely U. Member Spotlight

George Jacobs

You've had a long and lustrous career in the marketing and advertising world. What are some of your favorite unique and memorable experiences? Working with amazing brands and causes in New York. Meeting all kinds of celebrities at the Friars Club that I was a member of.

What do you do that brings you the most joy? I follow Jesus. Not Religion, but the Passion he brings to my life.

What is something you would like the Uniquely U. community to know about you? I will always be there to help with our students or faculty. I have been blessed through the years with wisdom to help people grow on their journey.

What is something you are struggling with at the moment? Sometimes health issue arise. But I never dwell on them. Instead I pray and conquer them.

What is one of your favorite quotes? *"You can never get caught in the Truth."* ~ me

What advice do you have for your 18 yr. old self? This is a hard one since everyone has their own journey to follow. You can do it on your own, but it's better to have faith. Crazy Faith.

"The moon is too heavy; can you help me carry it?"

Interviewing my dear friend George has me thinking about my best friend in 5th grade, MB. She had a summer house in Quogue (on Long Island, NY), which is where George lived when I met him. MB was such a great girl. Beautiful, kind, curious. I remember our many adventures playing at her summer house, going to the beach club and feeling so free and myself with her and her family. I didn't realize it at the time, but I think I connected with her back then because I longed for her family structure. To my young eyes, it was what it seemed like it was supposed to be (parents still intact and in love and present, lots of siblings and antics, etc.) One night when we were out in Quogue, she said I was clearly talking in my sleep, and it was the funniest thing to chat about the next day because I had zero recollection of even the dream I was having! She said that I was asking her to help carry the moon, that it was too heavy, and I needed help. My sweet, 10-year-old brain. Life was so innocent back then. By the time we were in 6th grade, everything shifted, and I sabotaged this beautiful relationship because I think it got too hard for me to be on the outside of what I deemed to be an ideal life. (If MB ever reads this, I hope she knows how much I appreciate her to this day.)

This is coming up because, man, doesn't the world just seem so heavy right now? From things so far outside like government and healthcare systems breaking down, to experiences so close to home like the worst, most traumatic loss of life, it feels like I am in a carnival game and have to keep shooting down all the fears that pop up with a BB gun. I know this is not just happening to me. We are ALL experiencing these weighty situations in one way or another and it is getting closer and closer to home.

But here's the thing...

I downright refuse to get stuck under the weight of it all.

Through this experience of building Uniquely U., I've connected with some extraordinary, beautiful, brilliant people who have been helping me see sense in all of this, so forgive my regurgitation of some of these concepts, but I feel the truth and helpfulness of them in my bones. These understandings are for me and my family and what we are currently dealing with. Hopefully they will help you, too.

The weight or darkness or satan or whatever you personally call it feeds off despair, anger, frustration, anxiety, fear, depression, guilt, etc.

The only way to combat the darkness, and make no mistake, we ARE at war for the very soul of this planet, is through love, kindness, trust, faith, compassion, and light—lots and lots of light from within our very being.

When something tragic happens that affects you, honor the pain and sadness that comes from your broken heart. By allowing tears, acknowledging the hurt, and grieving fully, you survive it by walking through it. You come out the other side with an understanding of the lesson, faith, and respect for yourself, and compassion for all involved.

Conversely, when something tragic happens that affects you and you avoid it by numbing yourself with substances, food, avoidance, etc., the guilt, fear, and anger will overcome you, and you will be stuck in the darkness.

When you are feeling sad or low vibe or dark or down, whatever you call it, find the simplest of joys in the moments to help you find your way out of it. These are some of the things I am doing today to help me through it:

- Light an incense stick that my neighbor Frank gifted me.
- Use my new, Molin+Goetz pepper-mint shampoo.
- Take the day off work.
- Journal (which is what these updates essentially are, right?)
- Hug my kids.
- Tell Dave I love him as many times as I can.
- Talk to Dana for 2.5 hours (ha, sorry, not sorry!)

These are extraordinary times we are living in. The world is changing before our very eyes and being aware of it is beautiful. But it does hurt. "No pain, no gain!" Isn't that what athletes say? Or my favorite from my mother when I was probably in 5th grade "You have to suffer to be beautiful!" (as she brushed the tangles from my always knotty hair). Must we feel pain to gain? Must we suffer to see and feel beauty? Maybe. Suffering and pain have always led to my own personal mini enlightenments. But the more practice I get, the shorter the pain and suffering and the greater the gains and beauty, and so it goes.

As I integrate the lessons of all of the experiences just within the last three days that have triggered my every fear imaginable, I feel like a warrior standing on a mountaintop—bruised and heartbroken, but empowered and resilient. I'm not ready to put down my spear, for the battle may be won but the war is ongoing. But I do feel a new sense of urgency and purpose to get Uniquely U. going, no matter what the outside circumstances dictate. THIS is what brings me the most joy and, well, life is simply too short and too wonderful to waste any more time.

For anyone that has made the leap of faith, I would really love to hear your stories and glean some inspiration from your experiences. It'll really help me carry the moon.

"But today the way I play the game
has got to change, oh yeah
Now I'm gonna get myself happy"
Lyrics from the son *Freedom '90* by George Michael

Uniquely Yours,
Angela DiMarco, *Founder/CEO*

In retrospect: I wasn't going to interject this story with present-day commentary, but I feel it is really important to put some context to the events that transpired that I mentioned at a very high level in this email because it was such a pivotal moment for me.

On the Sunday prior to this particular email, the body of a young girl from our town, who had been missing for several weeks, was found very far away from home. It was a national story and even though I didn't know her or her family, our town and the school district where my daughter was in 11th grade was entrenched in it.

The day prior to this email was actually the worst day of all. My daughter's friend had died by suicide. A sweet, polite, handsome boy who just entered the high school as a 9th grader. It was just so incredibly tragic. Me, my kid, my town—we were all just one, giant broken heart.

I also found out that my daughter was silently suffering from her own pain, and with the help and counsel of Dana getting us through it, I learned how to be the mom that Mattie needed. What I was bringing to the table was only what I had ever known, and it was just not good enough. Dana taught me how to communicate with my teenager, how to support her through this tragic event in her life, how to meet my own needs, and how to remain rational even when my brain was screaming fear-entrenched, irrational beliefs.

Much like losing my angel baby Joshua, this moment in my life was a catapult for what was to come.

In loving memory of
Christopher Coluccio & Gaby Petito

Uniquely U. Update #35

"Home is a place we all must find, child.
It's not just a place where you eat or sleep.
Home is knowing. Knowing your mind, knowing
your heart, knowing your courage. If we know
ourselves, we're always home, anywhere."

~ Glinda the Good Witch from the movie *The Wizard of Oz*

Happy Wednesday, Friends!

True to the duality of our lives, last week's update was coming from such a place of heaviness and tragedy, so this one's chock full of good news and good vibes!

Time to Pre-Game!

Back in the old days, the term "Pre-Game" (or pre-ing) meant something a little different from what I am about to tell you. I am laughing thinking of pounding cheap beers before heading to the bar (unless we were hitting up Nickel Beers Night at Tijuana's in Tampa, FL, but that's another story for another time.)

So, check this out...we've received another big investment chunk and are now scribbling the game plan on the chalkboard in preparation of kicking off the development of Uniquely U.! A few things need to happen so that I am in a position to give Uniquely

U. the 110% it needs and deserves, but thanks to a very generous investor, someone who unequivocally believes in what we are building, we are pre-ing and psyched!

I'd like to take a moment to thank each and every one of you for reading my ramblings each week, for your curiosity and anticipation for this platform, for your support as a friend. Some of you have been around for the full 35+ weeks of emails, some of you jumped in halfway, and some are new to the party. Either way, if you are reading this email right now, then please know you are important, you are appreciated, and you are loved. Once we kick off development, your input will be greatly appreciated. More to come on that...

U-Instructors — Deadline Tomorrow September 30th

After tomorrow, I will be closing the application window and finalizing our roster list for our first string, A-Team U-Instructors! In a few weeks, I'll be hosting a zoom orientation and preparing for 1-on-1s. I will be included in these as a U-Instructor for my branding workshops, and I am so excited to go through our vetting and training process!

The A-Team will be the first to meet my leadership team and a select few will have the opportunity to start earning income through beta workshops. In the meantime...

We're movin' on up!

On a personal note, we have been cleared to close on our home! It is literally a 5-minute walk from our apartment that has served us so well over the past couple of years. It has been a very twisty, very cluttered road to get to this place where I sit today. No matter what four walls are around us, I feel such a sense of peace, contentment and love with Dave and the kids. This house is just a representation of our expansion and connectedness as a family, and it also will help me get back to nature because the yard is huge and gorgeous! We get to stay in our beloved community and Mattie gets to stay in the same school with her amazing group of friends. I'm so excited for this next adventure being a homeowner with Dave!

For the next couple of weeks, the move will be my focus because I want to revel in the joyful feelings that surround this transition. Once we settle in, everything else will be set into motion. My goal is to launch **Uniquely U. Lite** in six months, so please continue to stick with me because things are about to get interesting! As always, if you need anything, don't hesitate to reach out to me. I'll just be over here clicking the heels of my ruby slippers together saying,

> "There's no place like home!"
> ~ Dorothy from the movie *The Wizard of Oz*

Uniquely Yours,
Angela DiMarco, *Founder/CEO*

Uniquely U. Update #36

Sent: Wed, Oct 6, 2021, at 12:00 AM

This is it, friends!

We are closing tomorrow, Thursday, Oct 7th at 1pm and we are officially moving our stuff on Tuesday next week! This apartment has really served us well for the past few years, even through months of being on lockdown when we basically built Christian a playground in our living room! So many memories, some tragic and some so beautiful and special. Uniquely U. was born here! Uniquely U. is about to take its first steps, perfectly timed with walking in our new home where we all have room to expand. I can't wait to share pictures with you!

Tuesday Night Packing Confessions

I actually like packing. Shhh, don't tell Dave or he won't want to help me, but I love getting rid of things that I really don't have a use for or finding that 'Oh I forgot I had that!' item. As I wrap each mug and party platter, I just can't help but fantasize how it will be used in our new home.

Tonight, while the family sleeps, I threw on this sexy mud mask and some 90's love songs and am just having the time of my life! I am also kind of hoping someone will wake up, so I can scare them with a Mrs. Doubtfire *"Heeeeeellllooooooooo!"*

Where were you when Facebook fell (for a blip in time)?

Did any of you notice or care that Facebook and Instagram were down for half the day yesterday? I found it very interesting as I observed my reaction. I was actually relieved, which speaks to my self-discipline over my endless scrolling, which is usually a procrastination tactic steeped in a little FOMO (Fear of Missing Out). I was also intrigued to observe how society reacted to it, and the feeling I got was that we are so resilient and will roll with the punches, no matter how hard those punches are! I do feel there was a collective sigh. Much like the lockdowns forced us to be more together, this very brief reprieve forced us to engage with the real world and to again look at our behaviors and patterns. It also made me REALLY excited for my friend Diane's new community platform to become live—it is going to be an amazing resource for all of us to stay connected with our local communities.

To our amazing A-TEAM, First String U-Instructors
(you know who you are!)

We are making big plans to connect with you soon and get you guys moving! I just have a few ducks to line up first, including reaching out to my brilliant General Counsel Tim Wan, Esq.! If you have any questions, please do not hesitate to reach out.

There is so much going on with Uniquely U. that I want to share with you, but it will have to wait until we are settled in our new home because I just want to revel in these beautiful, precious moments. Therefore, I will be skipping next week's update. In the meantime, if you need anything at all, please email, text or call me. And if social media goes wonky again, know that you are connected to us here at Uniquely U. We will always look out for your best interests and help light your way in the darkness.

Side note: I was just scrolling through the list of your email addresses and there are so many of you that I would love to just sit and have a virtual coffee catchup with! Ah, if only there were more time. If you are reading this, then, "Hi! What's happening in your world? How are your projects going? Are you happy? I am grateful to know you!"

Awe shucks—no one woke up in my apt! I suppose I should go clean this stuff off my face and get to sleep myself. Sweet dreams. I'll catch up with you in two weeks from a new location!!

"So, gather up your jackets,
move it to the exits
I hope you have found a friend
Closing time, every new beginning
Comes from some other
beginning's end, yeah"

Lyrics from the song *Closing Time* (at Dunder Mifflin)

Uniquely Yours,

Angela DiMarco, *Founder/CEO*

Uniquely U. Update #37

I will share more photos in the coming weeks, but above, in order, is our first rain and homecoming parade that passed right in front of our house, my first morning cup of coffee on the back deck, the view of our backyard from the second floor and my new lunch spot on the front porch in the swing chair with complimentary leaves casually falling from the trees on our property.

Hello Friends!

So, how are you doing? What's been going on in your world these past two weeks? I am rested and ready to catch up!

Moving is not for the faint of heart, I tell you! Especially trying to move with a toddler and a high schooler, but here we are living to tell the tale! And friends, I am head over heels in love with our new four walls. Everywhere I look, I get a flutter in my heart. This home has brought us so much joy, and it has literally only been one week! The important stuff is unpacked. The furniture is getting there. Some meals have been cooked. And most of all, we have all rested our heads comfortably and cozily for seven nights now. I am HOME. And I am ready to get to WORK!

Speaking of work...

Some of you know that I have been maintaining a full-time position with a local company. Well, today, October 20th, just shy of one year conceiving the idea for Uniquely U., I gave my notice! I've jumped off the cliff, and I am ready to soar into this new role of building this platform for you! By December 1st(ish) I will be full time Uniquely U., and the general plan is to have this platform up and running by April 1st, 2022—our web development team is getting ready to roll up their sleeves!

First String, A-TEAM U-Instructors:

I am almost ready for you all! The team has been working behind the scenes to prepare for your orientation and course development. Look for an email from me early next week with the details for your orientation date and time. This is the most exciting step in this whole process because YOU are the heart of U. I can't wait for the world to see all that you have to offer!

If you did not make the Sept 30th deadline to be on the first string, you can apply for the waitlist.

And now for some musings (did you miss them?)

You know, that saying, "Home is where the heart is" is ringing so true to me. I actually loved our little apartment, even though it lacked so much of what we would have liked to have. It afforded us the opportunity to have a safe, pretty roof over our heads during the pandemic. It allowed us to save for this house. Memories were created there. UNIQUELY U. was created there! Fortunately, memories stay with us no matter where we live. My point is, because my life is so beautiful at every angle, I see the beauty everywhere I look and roam. That little apartment could not fit us anymore because we as individuals and as a family unit are expanding exponentially, and now we have the space to stretch our wings and fly to new heights.

There has been a shift in me, and it is all happening in perfect, divine timing. Leaps of faith are becoming easier and easier as I take more. Trusting myself. Trusting my partners. Trusting the inner guidance and wisdom. I am on cloud nine! Come on in, the water is FINE!!!!!

Great things are closely in store for all of us!

Keep tuned to this channel for more exciting news and have yourself a fantastic week!

Uniquely Yours,
Angela DiMarco, *Founder/CEO*

Uniquely U. Update #38

Sent: Thurs, Oct 28, 2021, at 2:25 PM

> "It does not matter how slowly you go
> so long as you do not stop."
> ~ Confucius

Dear Friends,

Apologies, I missed sending my update out yesterday. I am finally getting a taste of being a parent to a teenager, and it's such a mix of heartbreaking, empowering, life-changing emotions. I say 'finally' because I have been oblivious to my daughter's pain and coping mechanisms up until a few days ago. The beauty of this is that we as individuals and as a family have a fighting chance to switch things up and come out on top. But it is really, really uncomfortable. But such is this magical thing we call life!

It has been one week...

...since I gave my notice at the day job. It is company-wide news now, and while my bosses are not happy, they cannot begrudge me the opportunity to start a business. I have handled the situation with integrity for myself, not them. I can walk out of that place with my head held high, knowing that I didn't screw them over. I gave them 5-6 weeks' notice, am helping to find my replacement, and am wrapping up what I can so they can have as painless a transition as possible. And then, in early December, guess what happens next?

All Uniquely — All the Time!

You guys have been extremely patient reading my musings that are essentially a placeholder for when I have some real company news to report. Well, that day is soon upon us! It isn't like I haven't been working on Uniquely for the past year (seriously, it has roughly been one year since the idea for this platform was jotted down on paper), but everything in my life has to have a certain amount of my time and focus in order for me not to feel overwhelmed or irresponsible. Myself and family always come first. Always. My new home had me for 100% for a little while there (kind of like I was on maternity leave-that's hilarious!) And then there is work. My day job has served me well for four years but now it's time to cut that tie and give this platform all I've got. Ugh, I can't WAIT for that day in December when I sit down at my new desk in my new home to work solely on my new business with my amazing team.

We ARE going to change the world.

By helping those find their spark and by helping them to shine their lights, others will join them. It'll be like that scene in *When Harry Met Sally* and Rob Reiner's mother says, "I'll have what she's having." You don't have to be a U-Instructor, either. Just by being a member of the community, connecting with one new person over a common interest, participating in events that will be free to all members...these are the magical ingredients we are adding to our witchy brew that will truly make a difference.

May your Halloween be filled with no tricks, only well-deserved treats and lots of laughs!

Uniquely Yours,
Angela DiMarco, *Founder/CEO*

Uniquely U. Update #39

Sent: Wed, Nov 4, 2021, at 4:15 PM

Hello Friends!

I don't know about what is happening in your corner of the world, but here on Long Island, New York, the chill is in the air—you can see your breath in the frosty morning. And the low, golden sun makes the changing leaves so vibrant! This season is definitely my jam. What is the weather like where you are?

Uniquely U. is gearing up!

With my impending 'last day' at the day job just a couple weeks away, I have been busy getting the ducks in a row to make this my full-time gig. The enormity of this opportunity is not lost on me. What was merely a thought one year ago is something that is now a real business! We have all the funding we need to get started because people believe in what I'm trying to build here. I am not used to having this level of support, respect and trust from someone other than my husband, and I am just learning to accept the love with gratitude.

So now that the money is raised and the job has been given notice, it's time to roll up my sleeves. The U-Instructor Orientation is set for Sunday, November 14th. 28 U-ROCKSTARS are warming up to bring our community some AMAZING courses! This group is really special because they have basically signed up sight unseen and will really have a lot of input on how this platform is going to work. I cannot wait to be in the same (Zoom)room with these people next Sunday! I have some other announcements to make, but my first-string A-TEAM U-Instructors get to hear them first.

Deep thoughts...

I am going through a very intense period of personal and spiritual growth. I think I need some of that precious down/quiet time to integrate everything I am learning. A lot of my experience has to do with changing old behavior patterns and moving away from fear and moving towards love and light. I believe this is happening for all of us collectively. Like living the 'Bird Box' movie— seriously, art imitating life! Our own brands of fear and trauma are bubbling up to the surface and we are being faced with choices...do we use the same old coping mechanisms and stay uncomfortable, anxious and fearful? OR, do we look at the root of the behavior, forgive ourselves for not knowing any better at that time, recognize how our behaviors are a result of that trauma and do something to change our behaviors? I am really trying to choose the latter. It isn't easy, and it isn't for the faint of heart. But those that choose to move towards love are WARRIORS and WARRIORS are my people.

Thank you to the badass WARRIORS for showing me the way every day (you know who you are).

Go hug *your* WARRIORS! Their choices and actions aren't easy!

Uniquely Yours,

Angela DiMarco, *Founder/CEO*

Uniquely U. Update #40

Sent: Wed, Nov 10, 2021, at 9:33 AM

Christian on the laptop, Mattie on the monitor, both about 10 months old!

Hello from my little corner of the world!

I sat down at my desk this morning with my hot cup of coffee ready to take on the day, and I just had to pause and take a breath and acknowledge the wave of gratitude that rolled over me. Here I am in my new, amazing, couldn't be more perfect home, sitting at my adorable new desk WITH drawers (I have not had a desk with drawers at home ever! I always sat at dining room tables or makeshift desks. This is HUGE!), overlooking my enchanting backyard with the morning sun streaming through the trees and listening to the birds chatter. This moment is so special, and I want to share it with you as a thank you for being here with me aboard the Uniquely U. train. Woot, woot!

What's your take on Facebook — ugh, meh or Yay!?

I am in the 'meh' category. I used to really enjoy seeing what my friends were up to, sharing pictures of my kids, venting or connecting with like-minded people. But then the cadence of Facebook shifted to being judgey and polarizing, so I stepped back from the personal stuff and just participated in groups with an occasional friend or family interaction. I could take it or leave it at this point, honestly. This is why I am going to build a closed social aspect to the Uniquely U.niversity eCampus. It'll take the best of what is out there so members can feel safe to interact authentically and connect with fellow students and U-Instructors on topics that matter to them.

But until that is built, I've chosen to utilize Facebook Groups (free—can't beat that!) Up until now, the group has been relatively quiet with the same few people interacting and keeping the blood pumping. But now that Uniquely U. is about to fire on all cylinders, I encourage anyone in our community who is on Facebook to interact and let people get to know you. Share your art, your music, your business, your passion, your journey—whatever makes your boat float! It's time for your voices to be heard, for friendships to be forged and for passions to thrive!

I've updated the group 'rules' which are more guidelines on how to post your content and interact in a new, helpful way:

U-Matter! We want to hear from YOU with your content, not something you are simply sharing from someone else. The best way for the community to get to know you is by you being authentically yourself.

U-Meme? If you find something you absolutely want to share that iss someone else's content, do so with some reflection and insight, i.e., "This inspired me because..."

U-Means-Business... Self-promotion is encouraged but please share why your business is beneficial to the community and provide offers that add value.

Engage. Engage. Engage! Be responsible with your content. If people comment, respond. Ask questions. Get to know each other. Find your people. This is the foundation of what Uniquely U. is all about!

Join us and invite your friends!

FYI, if LinkedIn, Pinterest, Instagram, Twitter or any other social platform are your jam, don't worry—we will become more visible when the time is right.

A-TEAM U-Instructor Orientation
Sunday, November 14th 12pm EST

Oh my goodness, friends...I am SO excited...I'm too excited! I can't wait! This very first orientation of the first string, A-TEAM

U-Instructors means GAME-FREAKIN-ON! This will be the first day of Uniquely U.'s life. Up until now, it has been a concept, a plan, a dream...but on Sunday, it becomes a reality! This is HUGE! See you awesome party people then!

Settling in is so satisfying.

I stayed up last night and unpacked all of my Great Grandma's china and crystal that my aunt let me borrow. I set it up in my mom's china cabinet that she saved for me when she sold her house on Pine Street. Dave and I recovered the dining room chairs to infuse our own style, which we are still figuring out. As I put the china away, I couldn't help but think of all the delicious meals my Great Grandma prepared and shared with family and friends, and I am so excited to continue that tradition. I love cooking and more so, I love creating memories.

The paradox of settling into my physical home and settling into my continued spiritual growth is really interesting. It's the same process: reflect on the past, appreciate the good, heal the hurts, create new ways and styles of being, and try not to repeat the old patterns that didn't serve me. I feel so much pride (they don't call them growing pains for nothing!), so much gratitude (I mean, just look at my office view and my beautiful, healthy family!) and so much love (for every teacher, friend and lesson). I hope you are enjoying your journey as well.

Uniquely Yours,
Angela DiMarco, *Founder/CEO*

Uniquely U. Update #41

Sent: Wed, Nov 17, 2021, at 1:26 PM

Hello Friends!!

For this week's update, I created a little video to announce my leadership team! Meet and connect with them on Facebook.

TRANSCRIPTION: "What's up Uniquely U.! I just wanted to share a little bit with you guys. We had our orientation on Sunday for our U-Instructors, and it was amazing and informative, and it is giving me so much insight on how to develop the process for everybody moving forward. What an awesome group of people! So many great questions. I'm just super excited!

The content, the people, the energy, it's all fantastic! It's like the beginning of something freaking amazing. I did share with them my leadership team, and I wanted to take a moment to introduce them to all of you because these are the people who are going to help us build this thing and just make it amazing.

There are three people I'm going to announce. The first person is my Director of Marketing, my pied piper, my go to guy–George Jacobs. George and I have a long history of working together. He is brilliant. He is sweet. He is kind. He is everything that we need to help us attract new members, new instructors, all that wonderful stuff. Say "hi!" to George–you'll be hearing more of him and from him as we develop the platform. Right now, George is sort of in the background but he is very, very important and very there.

Next, I consider these two women my left and right angel wings because I feel like they can just fly me up, and I have full faith that they will handle and do everything. With them onboard, I'm totally safe, and I trust them completely.

So, the first person is Cristen R. Grajeda. She has come to us with a lot of experience that sets her up for being a total support for you guys. She is my Director of Culture Enrichment · Global Support, and what that means is she's here to engage you guys, get to know you, survey you, be your support and your resource to create events and wonderful things that will bring us all together and keep us having so much fun.

She is also going to be global support, which means that she's here for you—she's here for you one on one, she's here for guidance, she's here for support. Whatever it is you may need on a personal level, Cristen is going to be your go-to, and she is incredible. She has a wealth of experience. She's a left brain/right brain professional, intuitive, and beautiful soul. I'm just so proud to be able to offer Cristen to you guys because it's what Uniquely U. is really all about—helping everybody become their best self and find their light, and Cristen is sure to fill that role. She's nicknamed The Light Keeper, and she will be hosting events at The Light House on Uniquely U., which is really, really fun and cool. So, feel free to connect with Cristen and say "hi!" on Facebook. Her alter ego is Shiva Raine.

Then my right wing, my consigliere, my intuitive guide, my oracle, my clairvoyant, whatever you need to call it. You guys know Dana Sardano. Not only have we been friends for years, not only did she invest in our business and really believes in what this is going to be, Dana has agreed to come on as my Vice President, my right hand, my everything, but on the other side of that, she's also going to be our Chief Officer of Content + Curriculum. Dana was a career educator, working with the school administration, developing programs, and working with students with special needs. She has so much experience that I still don't even know what to say–she just brings so much to the table that is like that missing piece that I didn't have. I knew I wanted to help the new U-Instructors be the best that they could be, but I didn't know how that was going to happen and then in walks Dana.

Dana is going to help you guys shape your courses, and she's going to help build our content library. She sees all the little nuggets and can help pull them out and give you the courage and the information so that you can present your work in the best way possible. To know Dana is to love her. Connect with her if you haven't yet.

Between George, Cristen, and Dana, my core team of leadership, I am just so excited! I have about two or three weeks left of working the day job before I do this full time. We've got the web development team–Scopic is lining up, and we're going to start building this thing–this is happening!

So, what I want to close with is this–if you feel like there's some kind of interesting thing happening here for you, but you're not sure where it is or what it is or how you fit in or how this is going to help you, just stick around for the ride. When the moment is right, you will know where you belong here. Just know that we're here for you, and we are ready. We're like, "come on!" but you just have to say, "I'm a team player," and there will be a place for you–whether you're a student, or you just like hanging out as a member on campus and getting to know everybody, going through the content library, like listening to music and streaming audiobooks or viewing beautiful artwork and watching videos that people have created for us. It's going to be an incredible environment for anybody who wants to be here. You can be a browser. You can be a fully integrated kind of person taking workshops and enjoying the events, or you can teach. Either way, is going to be amazing!

We've got such a good structure set up for you guys that will help YOU be successful. So, I'm just so excited to have my leadership team now out in the open. I've been working with them in the background for a while, and now it's all out there. The closet doors are open. If you need anything, if you have any questions, please email me, message me whatever it is, friend request me if we aren't friends yet.

I'm not very active in the Facebook world anymore, but I am in our Facebook Group until we have our social situations set up, which is going to be a couple months from now, but anyway stick around. There will be more exciting things happening and thanks for watching. I'm so glad you're here."

First U-Instructor Orientation was AMAZING!

Thank you to all who participated and who watched the replay. It was a LOT of information, and so many great questions were asked that will help me shape orientations moving forward. Great things are in store for our U.niversity!

What, no musings???

No, not this week. Business is taking off, so there is a lot of work that needs to be done. I'll just leave this song here for the Pink Floyd fans.

"Remember when you were young,
you shone like the sun...
Come on you raver, you seer of visions
Come on you painter, you piper,
you prisoner, and shine"

Lyrics from the song *Shine on You Crazy Diamond* by Pink Floyd

Shine on, you crazy diamonds!

Uniquely Yours,

Angela DiMarco, *Founder/CEO*

Uniquely U. Update #42

Sent: Sat, Nov 27, 2021, at 12:09 AM

> "I'm thankful for my family.
> I'm thankful for my friends.
> I'm thankful for the things I have.
> The thank yous never end.
> What are you thankful for?"
>
> Lyrics from a children's nursery rhyme called *The Thank You Song*

Hello Friends!

This week's update comes a bit late because we just hosted 22 adults and children for Thanksgiving, and it was a great success but a lot of work! I was going to share a pic of Dave and I and our delicious turkey, but I don't want to make the vegetarians or vegans cringe. I don't know if you have heard of the new children's YouTube phenomenon called Cocomelon, but in our house, it is a huge hit with my 3 year old Christian. The catchy tunes really have wonderful messages for him. This particular song quoted above has been swimming in my head all week, so you're welcome for the earworm if you choose to listen :)

Since the idea of what we are celebrating on Thanksgiving in the U.S.A. really has a dark overlying message, I choose to focus instead on how this holiday is the kickoff to a magical time of year. For about five weeks, I find that people are a little jollier. They express more gratitude and take time to think of and reconnect with distant family and friends. New and old traditions are established. Cookies are baked. Homes are decorated. I particularly love the many 'paid time off' days for holidays, as I have very little guilt leaving the office in the back of my mind for a few glorious days. All of these positive thoughts swim around us and fill our worlds with good, positive vibes and it is highly contagious (in a good way! lol)

Yesterday, we took Christian to see his first movie in the theater! We saw Scholastic's *Clifford the Big Red Dog,* and it was adorable! Christian liked the movie and paid attention to maybe 70%. I loved the whole concept, and at the end, Emily Elizabeth tells a crowd that it is good to be themselves and unique, to which I admit I teared up. Fun fact: I worked on some awesome projects for Scholastic in my heyday as a Crea-tive Director, and when Mattie was in preschool, she would brag to her friends saying, "My mommy works for Clifford!"—proudest moment of my career!

In Business News...

I want to express my eternal gratitude for the A-TEAM U-Instructors who are helping me to build a solid foundation and structure for our future teams. Their input and patience have been so appreciated! I have been listening and adjusting and learning and developing all because of their generosity with their time, talent, and experience. I heart you guys big time! If you didn't open my earlier email, **kindly note that your U-Syllabus submission deadline is extended to Wednesday, Dec. 1st** .

Uniquely U. is and will be a collaborative, iterative process. The most important thing to me is that everyone feels safe and supported!

One more week of work, my friends and I'm 100% Uniquely U.!

#blessed!

Until next week, I hope you have many beautiful moments brimming with gratitude!

Uniquely Yours,

Angela DiMarco, *Founder/CEO*

Uniquely U. Update #43

Hello Dear Friends,

Fair warning...I am feeling full of musings this week. I think I need to get it out of my system because come Monday morning at 9am, this Uniquely U. party is getting STARTED! Future updates are going to be a lot more focused on the actual development of our courses, the platform, memberships, team, etc. They will look more like a mullet—business in the front, party in the back (hehe).

I don't know if many of you know about this, but almost two years ago, I lost a baby boy in my second trimester. It was the most excruciating time in my life. Joshua was 18.5 weeks in utero and was a fully formed, tiny human. We actually got to hold him. In retrospect, I am amazed at how the OB ER nurses handled the whole experience. One nurse kept chanting to me, "You are so brave" as she stroked my hair or held my hand. The hardest thing that day was walking out of the hospital without my baby.

As I grieved, I tried to find some solace by understanding that this painful experience was not in vain. It led me on an amazing journey of truly awakening my spirit. I found videos created by the adorable Aaron Doughty and was fascinated by all this esoteric stuff like manifesting and shifting timelines. Then about 9 months after I lost Josh, I signed up for Victor Oddo's group coaching thing, and man, did that do the trick! The friends I made (Hi guys!) and the things my mind opened up to—I started to wipe the fog away from my eyes and see things from an entirely new perspective!

At the very end of his course in Oct. 2020, Victor guided us towards discovering our soul's purpose. Besides a dream I had since my late teens to befriend and sing sweet harmonies with Eddie Vedder, I rediscovered my love for teaching. I thought I could do what Victor did but for branding/marketing for small businesses. I went online to look up *Brand Coaches* and wouldn't you know it, there are dozens of Brand Coaches out there, all hustling, all doing a great job with their own brands. While my knack for helping people find their brand's uniqueness and bringing that to light would've been the key to my success, competing with other brand coaches for business just didn't sound like fun. But then, in what only can be described as a strike of angelic inspiration, the concept for Uniquely U. was born!

Now, while this was happening, I had commissioned Dana Sardano to paint a portrait of myself, Mattie, Christian, and my angel baby Joshua. Dana finished it and sent the ginormous 36" x 36" painting from Florida to NY just around the time this concept came to me. I was so in love with the painting and the experience of working with Dana to create such an intimate and perfect memorial to my baby boy that I had booked an intuitive guidance session with her. At the end of the session, I read her my little blurb about Uniquely U. and yadda, yadda, yadda...this game-changing company is about to be born into the world!

In February 2021, I ran a beta workshop called "Brand DNA—Decoding Your U-Chromosome" where I met Dana's very good friend Michelle Golinski (one of our A-TEAM rockstar U-Instructors—what up, girl!). Michelle is an extremely gifted Spiritual Liaison, and she received this message for me when she connected with Joshua. Here's what He said (this message is for all of us):

There is a lot of work to be done, and certain circumstances had to occur to put things in motion. There has been a perfect storm for many to take action. My human birth mother included. This is just the beginning, but what a beginning it is. Wait until she sees and realizes what is really happening. She thinks she knows, but she cannot even fathom the magnitude of what has been set in motion. It is a gathering of minds, thoughts and beings of purpose that will have an effect on the world. This is a current gathering that will change, shift, develop...the goal, the intention remains: to change, uplift, enlighten and awaken the masses, the collective consciousness, to all vibrate faster and higher in order to assist in saving the world...

I learned through Michelle that Joshua's short mission was to be a catalyst for me to *wake up* and build our new form of education. As I sit here and review the timeline, just...wow! I am in awe of how much I have changed and grown over the past two years. Looking back, I can see where Joshua had his little hand in helping me move things forward from the moment he was conceived.

Last year, celebrating our first Joshua Day was really hard because every day leading up to it, I would say, *this day, we told everyone we were pregnant* or *this time last year, my belly was starting to pop, etc.* Earlier this week, I was acting quite edgy, and when I checked in on myself, I realized it was because Joshua Day was approaching. As I told Mattie about why I was crankier than normal, I had the realization that my last day of the day job and my old life is this Friday, which also HAPPENS to be Joshua Day (December 3rd)!

I got a really, *really* painful kick in the pants two years ago, and because I followed the light-filled breadcrumbs and didn't fall down a dark hole of grief and despair, I rose up from the ashes like a phoenix, and I can feel my angel baby's pride and joy for the outcome of his mission!

This year, Joshua Day (12/3 or 3/12, depending where you are in the world) is truly a day to be celebrated! I know he is with me all the time, guiding me, watching over his dad and siblings. He loves our new house, and his magic is all over this company. Do I wish my little boy was physically here with us and growing before my eyes? Hell yes. But I know that there is so much more than this human experience, which will seem like a blip by the time I see him again.

If you've made it to the end of this email, thank you for traveling back in time with me. Soon, Uniquely U. is going to be so much bigger, and these little intimate moments I share with you each week will be less and less frequent. I hope this particular peek into my window helps you see why Uniquely U. is so magical and why being a part of it with me is so, so special. Are you ready?

Uniquely Yours,
Angela DiMarco, *Founder/CEO*

Uniquely U. Update #44

Sent: Wed, Dec 15, 2021, at 12:30 AM

Down on a distant shore I dreamed today.
Vision was cloudy, and it was purple hazed.
I dreamed away—I dreamed to today.

Endless seas in front, they beckon me.
Sandy ground below, I lost my feet.
I slipped away—I slipped to today.

Now today is not like distant dreams.
It's so much better than I let it seem.
It's peace—sweet peace.
Love and peace—my love—my peace.

Lyrics from the song *Distant Shore* by Angela DiMarco (that's me!)

My Friends!

I apologize for missing last week's update, but my routine is all shaken up now that I am full time with Uniquely! And, because my joy meter is exploding almost every second, there is no desire to procrastinate to do the work that needs to be done, unlike at my last job. It's so funny...I have a leftover freelance project to do by Christmas for my old job, and I just can't seem to get it done! But I will. I always do.

For the past year, I've been finding and sorting all the various puzzle pieces of the big picture of this business model, making piles of common elements, and now I am having so much fun putting all the actual pieces in place! So, let me tell you all the things I've been doing for the past week...

- Met with my General Counsel and worked on some legal stuff.
- Ordered checks.
- We had our first leadership status meeting.
- I got a credit card for the business.
- I met with our development team three times now, and we've made such progress already.
- I actually cut my first payroll checks!
- I bought a PRINTER (you know it is serious when I put a big, ugly black printer in my cute new office!)
- And a bunch of other little things for the business.

The past year up until 12/3/21 was all planning and dreaming. Now we are building and actualizing!

(DANG that is fun to say!)

Dana and Cristen have been meeting with our U-Instructor A(mazing)-TEAM for Coffee Chats and the initial offering is going to truly be the embodiment of this platform, helping people find their unique factor in all they do. This group of rockstars are helping to pave the way for all who will follow.

George, Rob and I have been meeting with our web developer. Our team at Scopic is brilliant, and they are exactly the right peeps to nurture and create our platform. Every conversation leads to more clarity on how this platform will look and feel, which leads to more joy bursting out of my seams!

Dave and I have been digging in the finances of the business. We met with an amazing CPA, who I feel is really the right man for this business. I am bringing on a bookkeeper next week, and we met with a payroll company today to get that whole thing sorted out. The biggest hurdle for us to nail down is how to pay our U-Instructors who are international. But have no fear, the answers are very near.

We are building a solid and sound foundation. I am connecting and collaborating with the very best people who are in line with our energy and core values (#1 is simple—don't be an asshole!) I feel like every time I need something or someone, it or they simply appear as if this were guided by something bigger than my tiny humanness. And those who do not align with what we are building here simply fall away with no ill will, drama or fanfare.

At the top of this email, I posted lyrics from a song concept that I wrote that has been running through my head this past week. Last week, I had to do a lot of sacral chakra healing, which had me thinking about freshman year at U. of South Florida where I met Dana for the first time in this lifetime. My 18th year of life was a very tragic time, and the main feelings I can easily recall were loneliness and not feeling worthy of having my needs met.

When I wrote *Distant Shore*, I tapped into those feelings and my dreams for the life I truly desired.

Now, almost thirty years later, the life I have is WAY beyond anything my 18-year-old self could fathom! I have a beautiful relationship with my husband full of mutual respect and admiration. I have two healthy, wonderful children and an angel baby guiding us all. I am following my passion to connect people and help light them up as my job! I have incredible, supportive, magical friends and family by my side. My point to all of this is to say that no matter where you are in your life, you too can make this life beyond *your* wildest dreams! Whatever it is that will bring you joy is yours to behold. I am living proof! Honestly, when I was 18 years old, I felt so alone. I was a shit friend and an even shittier daughter. I was a failure at school—had zero direction for my life. I abused whatever substance was in front of me. My biggest joy was daydreaming about hanging with Eddie Vedder. Now? I don't want to even close my eyes and miss a single second of this glorious, amazing world I live in!

I love my job! I love my life! I love all of you so much! Now go and make today as amazing as you are!

Uniquely Yours,
Angela DiMarco, *Founder/CEO*

Uniquely U. Update #45

Sent: Wed, Dec 22, 2021, at 10:49 PM

I made a quick video for this week's update:

TRANSCRIPTION: "Hey Uniquely U.! I just wanted to take this opportunity to say that I hope you have a happy and magical holiday season. For me, this has probably been the most exciting. It's the first time in a new house. My kids have their presents hidden in a spot that is not a closet covered by blankets because I was in an apartment for a long time. I finally have a 'Santa spot', which is really cool. I'm working full time for you guys, having business meetings and team meetings and just building. What we are building is so cool! If you take all the pieces—a social network, a library full of great content, workshops—none of this stuff is ground-breaking or new, but the way that we're putting it all together is going to create amazing experiences for you guys.

I don't know how you feel, but every time I call my insurance company, for example, and I hear "Press one for this...Press two for that..." and there are no humans that you can get in touch with for anything that you need, Ugh! We're going to change that. We foster human-to-human connections that happen to be built on a digital platform, and that's really what makes us very unique. The training process for U-Instructors and content contributors is an entire human process. You submit your application, and you are, there-after, nurtured and supported by a team of experts who are going to meet with you and get you ready so that you can present yourself in the best light possible because your success is the most important thing to us. You're success-ful, we're successful, and not only successful presenting workshops and such, but successful in the magic that's going to happen in these workshops. I've experienced it. I know it's going to happen. I can almost guarantee it 99.9%.

The connections that you will make if you invest in just being yourself will be so gratifying–and what I mean by that is don't put on the airs of being something that you're not. This is a place to be raw, to be you, to find those things that are super exciting for you and connect with like-minded people who are just here to support you.

Nothing that we're doing is about stress–my entire MO is no stress, peace out, man! I tell the whole team that if we have to push our goals out, we're pushing out because we're not here to have anxiety. So, this is a great place where you can just go and relax and have a good time, have amazing experiences, and learn something new that you thought would never learn. It gives you an opportunity to teach something you thought you'd never have the opportunity to teach.

Let's say you're an amazing gardener, you could share your expertise with others that could benefit from your passion. I need someone who's an amazing gardener by the way because I now have a backyard with these raised garden beds that are gorgeous. I definitely need somebody to teach me how to garden, so if somebody wants to sign up, please, that would be awesome.

For those who are new coming in—we've got a lot of people starting to express interest in what we're doing—I just want to let you know in a long-winded way that we are creating human-to-human, real, connected, amazing, passionate experiences.

I hope that you will stick around for my business development updates. We're getting ready over here for our first day of school to be April 2nd 2022...That's really exciting! That's kind of our goal right now. If it's not, No worries, we're just gonna do the best we can to get there. Please stick around, please email me, ask me any questions. Also, you can reach out to the team if you have general questions.

So have a very, very happy, magical holiday season. I hope that your days are filled with gratitude and love, and I will see you in 2022 because school is closed as of tomorrow through January 2nd, so no update next week. But yeah, I love you guys, I love what we're building, and I can't wait to connect with you. Bye!"

Hello, my friends!

I am not a huge fan of videoing myself, it is really not in my comfort zone, but I feel it is important to share myself in a manner as if we were on a Zoom call, so those of you who are new can get to know me better. Expanding on some of the ideas I spoke about in the above video...

You know, we're all about REAL human-to-human connections.

It is what is truly lacking in this digital world we live in. Emails, texts, social media personas, voice automations, etc.—they are all so impersonal. But we are shifting that. From the moment a U-Instructor sends in an application, there are some pretty spectacular humans waiting with open minds and arms to nurture your path to success. We are also going to invest in having someone answer the phone when you call our general number instead of an automated operator saying, "Press 1 for Angela, 2 for Dana..." After the break, I will introduce you to our new *Human Connections Representative*—I am just thrilled with the newest member joining the admin team!

Uniquely U. curates *experiences*.

While we have a lot of features being built that are all out there in one form or another, no one is putting them together in one awesomesauce basket of fun like we are! When Dana, *VP/Chief Officer of Content + Curriculum*, and I were sorority sisters at U.

of South Florida, we had a blast! But the fun was short lived because I was walking through trauma and making very bad choices. Imagine having the opportunity to get back on a campus that is full of school spirit, amazing events, and truly special workshops and content in the library knowing what we know today! I'll have so much more appreciation and gratitude in my attitude, I can tell you that! On our eCampus, you will meet like-minded new friends from around the world, taking workshops on subjects that really make your heart sing, and attending virtual and in-person events (as soon as we are able). Members will have a voice and a say on the events we host, and even the early ones will have some input on the actual platform itself! How cool is that?!? It's going to be amazing... I can't wait!

Left Brain People + Right Brain Folks + Spiritual Seers

If you just jumped in on our Facebook group (welcome!), you will notice that we tend to have a lot of metaphysical, esoteric friends posting and commenting, and that might turn off those of you who are more left-brained or somewhere in the middle. Please stick around because there is such value in the relationships and knowledge that can be shared with one another.

Left-brained people—I am like you because I have a very savvy business mind. I've been a creative marketing professional for more than half my life, and I really like understanding people's psyche and motivations. I like learning new technologies and creating financial spreadsheets. I am going to be teaching a workshop on how to prepare your brand and content so you can build your own simple website. I am also going to teach about defining your brand DNA. Why am I telling you this? Because the right-brained creative folks are going to need our help getting their businesses off the ground, marketing themselves, sales training, social media advertising help, etc. All those things that you have the knowledge for and probably take for granted are real barriers to these friends reaching their next level.

Right-brained people—I am also like you because I am creative to my core. I have been doing graphic design since my real college days at SUNY Farmingdale (post USF). I love cooking, decorating my new house and making Halloween costumes for my kids. I write songs on my acoustic guitar and craft with Christian. Us right-brained people embrace the things in life that make our hearts sing. We are good at chasing our passions, and that is where we can help those left-brained people get unstuck. There will be some who come to Uniquely U. because they are just done with their careers and are searching for their purpose, and there will be some who are content with the day job but are looking for a little creative outlet to keep their motors running. We will be there for them to help flick that light back on inside!

Spiritual seers—I am also like you because I have had a long awakening and every day, my awareness of my inner and outer world expands. I understand and speak your language, and I connect with you on a higher vibration. Left- and right-brained people need us to help kickstart their awakening, to be guides on their spiritual journeys...but you already know that because that is why you are here!

See, there is a beautiful trifecta of support and connectedness that might not otherwise happen in your lives. Not only will you make new friends, but you will reach new audiences for your brands and businesses. Our job is to facilitate, support, and champion each of you and your incredible awesomeness!

With all that said, I'll wrap this up with wishes for a spectacular holiday season. Our school is on break from Dec 23rd–Jan 2nd, so I will reconnect with you all in the new year! Enjoy this time with your families and friends and get pumped for 2022!

I hope your holiday season is as magical as you are!

Uniquely Yours,
Angela DiMarco, *Founder/CEO*

Uniquely U. Update #46

Sent: Wed, Jan 5, 2022, at 10:42 PM

(cough, cough, covid)

Hi Friends,

First and foremost, a very, very happy 2022 to you all! I hope your holidays were wonderful and peaceful and restful! We were doing fantastic until Dec. 30th when Covid came and hit me like a mother. I woke up Thursday morning and had this insane chill through my core. Thank God for Mattie who helped get me warm and watch Christian so I could rest. I tested negative with a home test. Then the fever came and the aches. On Friday, I tested positive. Dave, who was negative still, took Christian to the pediatrician and he was positive. Mattie tested negative, but to be safe, she had to miss her friend's NYE party and, instead, be quarantined in our basement away from everyone. It was eventful! I slept right through the ball dropping.

On Saturday, Dave tested positive and luckily, I got a spurt of energy and was able to watch Christian while he fought the chills and aches. By Sunday, I was on my back again. Christian is perfectly fine and in fact happy to be home with mom and dad for a second week in a row (if I had the energy, I would be potty training him!) Dave is also better. It's just me still feeling like poop going on day 7.

Even though my chest feels like I've been swimming for days and my entire midsection aches like I was in a bullfight and the bull won, I can't help but feel extremely grateful for this time with my family in this forced shut down. I've had to truly let go and trust everyone else to take care of business while I lay around, which is really, really hard for me to do! But Dave is doing great at being a "Mr. Mom", and Mattie is getting herself up for school and homework done. Dana, Cristen and team are taking care of Uniquely U. There's nothing left to do but get better! I must say that I have the most amazing team! And hey, now I will have some natural born antibodies in my system!

By the way, *Queer Eye Season 6* on Netflix is by far the best one yet. Tears for days!

December was an interesting month for me. Transitioning from the full-time job working for someone else to working full time on Uniquely U. took a lot emotionally. Add hosting big family dinners in the new house and Christmas in the mix, it's no wonder that my defenses were down. I had very little time for self-care, and when the bug found its opportunity, it struck hard and fast! If you were like me and ran yourself a little ragged for the holidays, take some time for self-care now before you are forced to, too!

Those of you who are in the Facebook group, please do me a big favor and help the community stay engaged? Share experiences, ask questions, comment on one another's posts. It would make me feel better knowing that you are all keeping the dream alive, so I can convalesce.

I'm excited to get back to work. But not until I am fully recovered. And that's all the steam I have for you for this update. Peace out!

Uniquely Yours,
Angela DiMarco, *Founder/CEO*

Uniquely U. Update #47

Sent: Sat, Jan 15, 2022, at 11:43 PM

Hello Friends!

I am finally feeling better and more myself. I typically send my updates on Wednesdays, but I chose to take this past week slowly and do only what was absolutely necessary for the business and allow my body to rest and recoup. I've been doing a lot of emotional healing as well, which has left me overflowing with gratitude.

Let's start at the very beginning...

I was thinking back to Nov. 2020 when this idea for Uniquely U. was born. I had just completed a three-month-long group coaching course with Victor Oddo, learning how to listen to my intuition and find my purpose. At first, I thought my purpose was to teach marketing and branding to small businesses, but there were so many already out there doing a bang-up job that I just didn't feel like competing with them. Then this paragraph flowed from my pen like it was written through me. I know that will sound crazy to some, but I can't explain it any other way!

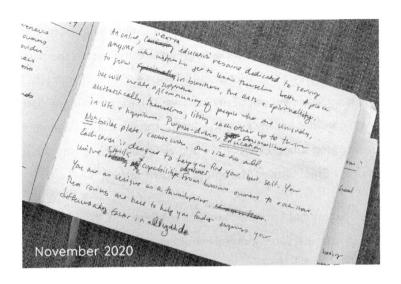

My journey of personal discovery led to the conception of this platform. It took almost exactly 12 months to go from idea to execution—to write the business plan, plan the finances and budget, seek funding, building the brand, learn as much as I could about running a new kind of company, build the team and finally leave my 25+ career as a creative marketing director just two months after buying our house to make the biggest leap of my life. At the very beginning, the only thing I needed was the courage to tell people my idea. I read from that page pictured above to a handful of people, and I remember answering questions about it, expanding on the idea with every conversation. But everything changed when I read this page to my old college friend Dana Sardano during an intuitive guidance session with her. At first, she was very quiet, and I thought maybe she thought it was a dumb idea or maybe too ambitious. But then she said something to the effect of, "you HAVE to do this. The world NEEDS this!" and that spoke to something in my core—an acknowledgement that I knew I was onto something. From that day, Dana has been the kicker of my pants, telling me the hard truths that only a true friend could ("You need to quit your job.") and helping me get out of my own way. I have joked in the past that I consider her my GAL-RU, but truthfully, she has been the unwavering support that I have and will need. This is why she is my VP / Chief Officer of Content + Curriculum.

And that is what I want Uniquely U. to be for you. Wherever you are in your personal journey—whether you are exploring your passions, self-bettering, or ready to make that scary career leap—we will be there every step of the way. We, as a collective community. We, as your admin team. We, as new friends from all walks of life. We are U. Everything you are experiencing has been experienced by someone here. I encourage you to stick around and find your people. You will meet and help people by tapping into your experiences and achievements, too!

Sounds great, but now what?

SO much is happening behind the scenes. The foundational stuff needed to start a company are all pretty much in place (I received my first ADP paycheck yesterday!) We are working with amazing people who are aligned with our vision. Marketing plans are being created, workshops are being refined, the web platform is being designed and our admin team is being trained. One of our most important core values is that this is a HUMAN platform. Don't you hate it when you call a company with phone automation (press 1 for this, 2 for that, 3 for the other...)?? I also don't like the term 'Customer Service' for us. At Uniquely U., we don't have customers that need servicing. We have humans that require connecting!

So, to that end, I'm thrilled to announce that we have recently hired my dear friend Charlie Singer to be our *Human Connections Representative*! He will answer the phone (when we get our number) or call you back. He will help you get to who you need to get to or find answers to your questions. Charlie is the best man for this job. Get to know him a little better in this month's U. Member Spotlight.

Uniquely U. Member Spotlight

Charlie Singer

What advice do I have for my 13-year-old self? Not everyone is going to like you, but the ones that do, if you are being your authentic self, will always be a part of your life.

What brings you the most joy? I love seeing people smile and being themselves, carefree, vulnerable and honest no worries in the world if I can help with that it brings me much joy.

What is one of your favorite quotes? "There are no ordinary moments."

What is something your most proud of? I never gave up; I have fallen so many times but I got up and kept going and I kept searching for the right answers for me.

What are you struggling with at the moment? I am a loyal person to a fault and learning to let go of people I love with all my heart, but I know they're not good for me and can't go where I am going.

Who or what inspires you lately? Me =)

Well, that wraps up this week's update. Remember, no matter where you are on your journey, if you have found yourself here with us, then you have found your team that will provide whatever you need to help you climb your mountain.

Have a great week!

Uniquely Yours,
Angela DiMarco, *Founder/CEO*

Uniquely U. Update #48

Sent: Wed, Jan 19, 2022, at 1:50 PM

"Have you been half asleep?

Have you heard voices?

I've heard them calling my name."

Lyrics from the song *The Rainbow Connection* by Jim Henson's Kermit the Frog

Hello Friends,

I want to share a very sweet moment that happened last night. I was singing lullabies to my little guy Christian, going through our usual playlist. His back was to me, and he was all snuggled and getting sleepy. The last song I sang was *The Rainbow Connection*, and at the end of it, he sat up, turned around and gave me an unprompted big hug and kissed me all over my face. He said, "I just love you so much!" and then rolled back over and drifted off to sleep. My heart was melting!

I shared this story with Dana earlier and she pointed out that Christian might've been moved by more than my glorious singing voice (I joke). Perhaps it was his higher self or someone else from another plane bringing to my awareness the lyrics I was singing and to take stock in what is happening in my life today. Because Christian's reaction was so uncharacteristic, this concept rings true.

I wanted to share this with you to show you how important it is to talk to people in your circle who 'get it' and have your best interests in mind. It helps to see beyond what is obvious and helps to move us forward. We move forward when our heart skips a beat because of a joyful moment. We expand when we fill our gut with a deep, empowering breath. We rise when we open our minds to new possibilities. Having a person or a community who understands this and encourages our success is the key to unlocking our new way of being!

This is the very essence of what I envision Uniquely U. to be for everyone involved, whether you are a student, a U-Instructor, or just a registered guest walking around the eCampus and chatting with like-minded friends in the Commons.

As I develop each feature for our platform with our amazing team over at Scopic, my heart skips that beat with excitement, my gut fills with empowered breaths, and my mind opens to all the possibilities, to all the people who will be helped by feeling these very same feelings! It's such a JOY to build this business on every single level! That all being said, we are working on refining our call to action to join Uniquely U. This is a working draft. We invite constructive critiques to help this resonate with those we are trying to reach and help. Please reply to this email with your thoughts. Even if you have no critiques and this message calls to you, we'd love to hear from you!

Uniquely U. Call to Action:

As the world appears to be crashing and burning right before our eyes, we often feel powerless and hopeless that there isn't anything that we as individuals can do to prevent the strife that is occurring all around us.

What we at Uniquely U. have learned is that the only answer to improving our global crises is to first improve ourselves. We may not have the ability to "control" what occurs in the macrocosm of our life experience, but we have 100% control of what occurs in the microcosm, and we understand that doing so begins with our own personal health and wellness.

We also understand that health and wellness are not just about green drink and treadmills; it's about understanding what WE want out of life and knowing how to get it.

We understand that each of us at the core truly desires love, joy, peace, and freedom, and we at Uniquely U. have created a community and a platform so we can achieve these states of being together!

If you...

- are tired of the status quo,
- no longer want to do as you are told by those who neither know you nor care about your best interests,

- feel like there is more to life than that bill of goods you were sold as a child—work-eat-sleep, rinse, repeat,
- are sick and tired of being sick and tired,
- feel trapped in an existence that no longer serves you and are unable to see your way out,
- value cooperation more than competition,
- value community more than separation,
- value love more than fear,
- desire to be seen and heard,
- want to feel love, joy, peace, and freedom,

...then Uniquely is the place for U!

Go to FindUniquelyU.com and join your community—we're ready and waiting to help you live joyfully!

"I've heard it too many times to ignore it.
It's something that I'm supposed to be."
Lyrics from the song *The Rainbow Connection* by Jim Henson's Kermit the Frog

Uniquely Yours,
Angela DiMarco, *Founder/CEO*

Uniquely U. Update #49

Sent: Wed, Jan 26, 2022, at 2:16 PM

Calling all U-Instructors!
Applications are now being accepted.
Submit by Friday, February 10, 2022
Click on the link for the application. Good luck!

Hello Friends!

I am so excited to announce that we've decided to open another recruitment round for U-Instructors!

APPLY HERE: FindUniquelyU.com *(If you have previously applied but it wasn't the right time for you, you're welcome to apply again.)*

For information on our different schools and to learn more about our U-Instructors, visit FindUniquelyU.com.

For those of you who've been following my emails for a while, you know that my taking time for myself to just be present and mindful hasn't been the easiest. I am always "too busy" running the household and the business. However, for the past couple of weeks, I've been adding a little me time in my morning to shift from the chaotic routine getting the breakfasts made and the family off on their way to what is next for me. With a hot cup of coffee in hand and my phone far away from me, I've been sitting on my couch (it is too cold here in New York to sit outside!) contemplating the trees in my backyard.

The many benefits of taking these 20 minutes include:

- Shifting my energy so I can be present with what is next.
- Me feeling less stressed and angsty, especially when Christian has a rough morning.
- Analyzing crazy or interesting dreams and what the messages could be for me.
- Thinking about Uniquely U. and what I can do to best serve the company for the day.

What I have been thinking of lately is how much Uniquely U. is like a tree. We are in the sapling stage, where our roots are firmly planted so we no longer need rope to support our new trunk. We have main branches with smaller branches, and we had leaves that fell during the autumn. If you look at us against the cobalt blue winter sky, you see that we have an identity (we are certainly a tree!), that we are strongly rooted and will make it through the winter, and that we are healthy and poised to grow beautiful leaves once spring arrives (maybe even fruit? It's a surprise!). Our roots and trunk represent the leadership team and business partners. The branches represent our U-Instructors, and the leaves represent our members. When leaves fall from a tree, they carry the wisdom of being high in the sky, absorbing AND providing nourishment to their branches, mingling with the birds and other critters. They either land at the bottom of the tree and bring that nourishing information to the roots, or they drift off with the wind and share the nourishing information with other trees and critters. Because every root, branch and stem have an important role in the cycle, the tree grows to its full potential. No one part is more important than the other. And that is why Uniquely U. is so much like a tree. We are creating an even playing field.

Everyone who is a part of this platform, from the member to the leadership team, is important. We hope you always feel heard and supported, no matter what your role is. For me, I can see our tree at its fullest potential, and it is magnificent!

I try not to think too far into the future, but it is hard for a visionary to stay present in the moment when planning and dreaming are so much fun!

So, it seems that I am developing a little morning ritual of my own to help me work on my presence. What are some of your routines or strategies that help YOU stay present? I would love to know!

Please share this message with anyone in your life who might be a good fit for becoming a U-Instructor. Thanks for nourishing our tree! Have a fantastic week!

Uniquely Yours,
Angela DiMarco, *Founder/CEO*

Uniquely U. Update #50

Sent: Wed, Feb 9, 2022, at 5:05 PM

Deadline is this Friday!

Applicants, please save the date for U-Instructor Orientation:

Sunday, February 13th at 10am EST

Hello Friends,

I didn't send an update last week because, well, let's just say that I had a HUGE learning week, and I just didn't have it in me to connect outside of what was happening. Plus, my full attention on the situation was imperative to me really growing and learning from it.

Since December, when I went all in on Uniquely U., I've faced a multitude of situations that challenge my "old me" behaviors vs. my "new me" ones on a daily basis. I had the biggest growth spurt this week because I truly integrated a magical ingredient to living joyful, content, and free. You want to know the secret? I'll tell you *all* about it (I feel so smart because I finally GOT it).

The secret to growing, expanding and living joyfully free is this...

Awareness. Seriously...that's it! How can you implement this magical ingredient to live a joyful and content life?

First, look at *everything* you encounter as an opportunity. The traffic jam that has you late to work could very well be so you can look over at the car next to you and get a much-needed warm smile from a stranger, or to see that thing on the side of the road that reminds you of a loved one who's passed. You're given the opportunity to transform your energy from 'harried' to 'present and content.' The key here is to not get wrapped up in the drama of the situation, but to step back and say to yourself, "What information is this situation giving to me? What can I learn from it?"

Second, recognize how you act or react to these situations and look for patterns that you've been playing out since child-hood. Taking the traffic jam for example, can you look back and see all the times you've been so hurried going from point A to point B? Think about what you probably missed because you were not fully present. If you look up the word 'frazzled' in the dictionary, you might find my picture next to the definition. A previous version of myself missed SO much because of my be-liefs that if I didn't get there on time or if I didn't get the project done perfectly, I'd let people down, and then I'd feel unloved and unworthy. From my preteen years to my mid-forties (hint, I am still in my mid-forties), this was (sometimes is) my way.

Third, be AWARE of your patterns [and there it is!]. Once you are consciously aware of your reactions to life, you can be sure that more challenging situations will pop up to help you hone your new, amazing skills of shifting out of your old patterns and beliefs! Every single day something tests my ability to stop and smell the roses, and if I am not careful, that old familiar, comfortable pattern of being hurried and stressed so I can prove my worthiness easily creeps back in. But it is getting easier to nip it in the bud because I am becoming more aware of the ick or uncomfortable feelings that accompany the beliefs and patterns that no longer resonate with my shiny new self.

Of course, there is work to do beyond that, but once you *know*, you can't *unknow*, and to be aware of something you want to change without doing anything about it just seems like self-sabotage, *ya know?*

I experienced so much personal growth in the last five days that I feel like I am at least two inches taller and 10 pounds lighter but with a hangover from it all. Whew!

In other news, it is REALLY fascinating to watch our platform start to take shape. It's like sculpting a hunk of clay and watching it turn into a masterpiece! Our team at Scopic Software is just the most amazing team ever—so talented, so kind, so much fun! I hope to someday be able to introduce them to you.

And I can't WAIT for the first day of school! I need to give a shout out to Dana Sardano, *VP/Chief Officer of Content + Curri-*

culum and Cristen R. Grajeda, *Director of Culture Enrichment + Global Support.* These two talented, amazing humans are curating content for Uniquely U. and working hand-in-hand with our U-Instructors to get them ready for the first day of school.

Dana and Cristen have created a truly ground-breaking onboarding process that sets our platform apart from anything out there. Our U-Instructors are people we get to know on a personal level. Through our Ready-Set-Teach! process, we learn about their needs and hopes, and we do everything we can to set them up for success. If you are interested in joining our team, please apply on FindUniquelyU.com by this Friday, Feb.11th, and save the date for the <u>U-Instructor Orientation on Sunday, Feb. 13th at 10am EST.</u>

It is looking like the first day of school will be in May now, instead of April 2nd as I had hoped, but everything is happening in perfect harmony, and the "new me" can calmly and happily go along with that.

Have a great week!

Uniquely Yours,

Angela DiMarco, *Founder, President + CEO*

Uniquely U. Update #51 — Last one for a while

Sent: Tues, Mar 1, 2022, at 4:36 PM

Hello Friends!

I have been writing these updates for a little over a year. One year! Crazy, huh?!?

I have to go below deck and tinker around with our development team, so we can get something up and running for you all in the next couple of months. This is the moment where we go from planning to creating—where the *real work* begins. My focus needs to be on lock so no time or money gets wasted. Plus, this is really the fun part for me (I'm going to embody my inner Tony Stark—for all you Marvel fans out there!)

When you see "**Uniquely U. Update #52**" in your inbox, I hope you'll be as excited as I am because I'll be announcing the impending launch of our platform!

The only reason I can do this is because of my team—my famiglia. These amazing humans believe in the vision of Uniquely U. so much that they are willing to do whatever is needed to support the development and growth of this platform. My gratitude cup is overflowing! Here is who you can reach while I am literally hunkered down in my basement:

Dana Sardano
VP/Chief Officer of Content + Curriculum

Most of you know who Dana is as a person, but who Dana has become for me and Uniquely U. is so clear and so important to my/our growth. I trust Dana with my life. We speak ad nauseum about the vision and our processes and our plans, and I know that if I were to kick the bucket tomorrow, Dana could pick up the ball and run with this. We are practically birthing this baby together! Her 25+ year career as an educator, administrator, and liaison to students and parents has poised her so perfectly for this role.

I am in awe of her every day, and her passion and enthusiasm are infectious (the good kind!). To that end, I have handed the reins over to Dana to manage all U-Instructors, Applicants and eventual Library Contributors. This includes overseeing all the steps in our amazing Ready-Set-Teach! process, corresponding with the team and just all things content-related. There is no one more qualified to lead our U-Instructors along the path of success (whatever their definition of success may be.) If you are interested in joining our U-Instructor team, please reach out to Dana. She's going to continually crush it and I am so proud to call her my consigliere, my sister and my best friend.

Cristen R. Grajeda

Director of Culture Enrichment + Global Support

And then there is Cristen...you guys, if you haven't had the chance to connect with this awesome human yet, please try to. Every time Dana and/or I meet with Cristen, our Uniquely U. world gets brighter and clearer. Not only is Cristen just the sweetest person on earth, but she is also brilliant and insightful.

As I envisioned, I wanted my role to be, but realize now that I can't do it all myself, Cristen is stepping in my shoes and is here for you all—for members, guests, administrators, U-Instructors, Applicants—to help everyone feel connected, respected and heard. True to her title, she understands and embodies our Uniquely U. vision and strives to help create a culture that is perfectly aligned with it. This is one of those "I could not have said it better myself" situations. To that end, I have handed the reins over to Cristen to connect and collaborate with those of you who want to be a part of what we are building here. She is your Light Keeper. In the coming months, as we build the platform and create new features, I am going to need your input and your insights to help shape the future of Uniquely U. You—who've been following along from the beginning or for a hot minute, who understand and see the enormous value of what we are building here—are who we want to hear from and work with. If Cristen reaches out to you, please reach back. I thank you in advance for your participation. It means the world to us!

And then of course, I have my reliable dudes in the background helping every which way they can so I can do the things I need to do.

My heart bursts with gratitude for:

- Dave DiMarco, *(a.k.a., my hubby) Director of Finance*
- Rob Sgambellone, *Director of Technology + Accounting*
- George Jacobs, *Director of Marketing*
- And the whole *team at Scopic Software*

Of course, I couldn't write this last update without a tiny little musing to leave you with.

I've been thinking a lot about what 'family' means to me lately. Relationships with blood relatives have their fair share of ups, downs, dramas, estrangements, etc. As you get older, you know who you can rely on, who is going to bail on a gathering, who you can talk to, who you can't, who installed your buttons and who pushes them, who is going to drop off food on your doorstep when you have Covid...there are a lot of knots in those ties that bind us. And thank goodness for the knots because without them, we might not learn and grow and become our unique, individual, amazing selves.

On the other side of the bloodlines lies our chosen family. People who we have no predetermined ties that bind, only ones we chose to loop onto. People who love us and we love so unconditionally, who are so supportive, so reliable that it makes our lives that much more joyful just by them being in it.

In all my growing up years, I thought I had "best friends" or relatively good relationships with others, but the truth is that they all suffered and lacked a sense of true connectedness because I was not yet connected to myself and wholly happy. Like attracts like, so there I was, lonely among a sea of friends, family and colleagues. I didn't give anyone a chance to know ALL of me, only the good bits that I thought they wanted to see.

But now that I know who I am and I know how and why I tick (for the most part), I've been aligned with some of the most amazing people who I call my chosen family.

First and foremost, my husband Dave is my rock. I used to be envious of what I deemed as 'good' and 'healthy' marital relationships that I read in books or saw in movies, never thinking it was possible for me. But Dave and I are the bestest of friends. We have each other's backs and no matter what, and we are on this ride called life together. Our family is his top priority. Never have I felt safer or more protected than I do with Dave. Plus, I think he's such a hottie!

I would be remiss if I didn't include Elle amongst my chosen family. Elle is a childhood friend of my mom and aunt and really has our family history down pat! She is such an extraordinary human who has lived an incredibly interesting life. She could keep you on the edge of your seat with her stories! For the longest time, I wasn't able to SEE like I do now, and now, I SEE Elle for the beautiful, supportive, light-bringing being that she is, and I am so grateful for her unconditional love and guidance. She gets it all, man—like, really GETS it—and it is so refreshing to connect with her.

And then there is Dana. Some of you may not know our story. We will get into the details another time, but briefly, it started way back in '92 when Dana was my sorority pledge mom my freshman year at USF, and back then, I looked up to this powerhouse chick and wanted to be just like her. I annoyingly acted like her too, but hey, I was 18! We lost touch for like twenty years and then really reconnected in the fall of 2020 when she painted a gorgeous picture for me and...yadda, yadda, yadda...she is now my business partner, my best friend, my GAL-ru, my confidant, and most importantly, my big sister (quite literally if you go back to our Sigma Delta Tau days!) Her husband Rob is seriously the most amazing 'brother-in-law' a girl could have. I love him so much and have such respect for him. Our families met up a couple weeks ago while on vacation and seeing our four kids play together and enjoy each other's company like cousins just made my heart burst!

I feel such an abundance of joy and love in my life, and it's honestly all because I did the hard work to get here. None of this was handed to me. I have had my share of enormously painful and traumatic experiences that I CHOSE to NOT let define me.

I CHOSE to hope and work towards a better way. My CHOSEN family is my reward, and oh, how freaking sweet it is!

Thank you so much for following along with my updates and musings. I don't like to project, but honestly, I can't WAIT to send you Update #52—my heart is already doing flips! I will temporarily leave you with this love song to all those who I love. See you in a couple months!

"Oh, I'm a lucky man
To count on both hands the ones I love
Some folks just have one
Yeah, others they got none...

I wonder everyday
As I look upon your face
Everything you gave
And nothing you would take..."

Lyrics from the song *Just Breathe* by Pearl Jam

Uniquely Yours,

Angela DiMarco, *Founder, President + CEO*

One month later...

Uniquely U. Update #51.1 —

Greetings from the underground!

Sent: Tues, Mar 30, 2022, via YouTube

TRANSCRIPTION: "Hi everybody, Angela DiMarco, I felt uncomfortable not connecting with you guys by not writing my updates, so if any of you missed my lengthy weekly email updates, this one's for you. I'm kind of coming up from the underground a little bit, and I just wanted to fill you in on what's happening.

We are in full swing developing our platform. It's a functioning, working, live thing, and now we're just fine-tuning and tending to the details.. By May, I should have something like really, really cool and tangible and will be able to announce our launch date. So please keep a lookout for some marketing messages because school is starting in June, and we have amazing workshops lined up with amazing new U-Instructors.

Dana and Cristen have been grooming everybody. We've got this awesome Ready-Set-Teach program—this whole training process that helps people get ready for being in front of the camera and being in front of a classroom. We've got technology training and all kinds of awesome stuff happening behind the scenes.

The plan is to start with the workshops, so we're gonna get you guys into the whole feel of it, but then we're going to continue developing once the workshops start. Then we're going to go into the next thing and then the next thing and then the next thing. I've got all these awesome features on the shelf, and we're going to be developing them one at a time. We're gonna be creating a social platform. We're gonna be creating a business directory for everybody. We're gonna be creating a library full of amazing content that's free to all members—just incredible things.

It's hard to put a lot of what we've been doing into words. I don't really say much about the features because up until like a couple weeks ago—it's just been planning, planning, planning, but now we are putting the foundation in, and we're almost at the point where we're decorating the walls. It's so awesome guys. It's so awesome!

Cristen is going to start reaching out to you guys or if you're on Facebook (Shiva Raine is her pseudonym.) Dana will be connecting with all the U-instructors. Even if you at one point submitted an application, attended the orientation, or were part of the process in any way, and it didn't work out, don't worry. Timing is everything, and you are always welcome.

Just know that, as a student or a member, whatever it might be, please know you're with us always no matter what. This is not a platform with 'hard feelings'; this is a platform with inspiration and excitement. So, know that we believe in you and want the timing and everything to be right for everybody. So that being said, please, don't feel bad if you we here with us from the beginning and now you're not; that's just life, and it's okay. We love you.

Yesterday, I talked to my old boss. For those of you who don't know, in my previous career, I was a Marketing and Creative Director for many years, and I resigned last December to build this platform that I believe in so strongly full time. It had been a bit of a rough transition emotionally because I hadn't realized how attached I was to that identity and my beliefs around that identity, so talking to him was cause for reflection.

We chatted for a bit, and the conversation created so much gratitude in my heart for having the courage to take that leap of faith. I came to realize that every day is exciting—even the difficult days and the stressful days, even the days that I doubt myself. Speaking to him reminded me that I did enjoy my old job, but even on my roughest days building this platform, nothing compares to this. Nothing!

So, if you are a person who happens to be on the cusp of making a change, just do it. Just do it because once you're doing something that brings you joy, everything conspires to make it work out for you.

And once we're up and running, we're going to have support for you—like if you don't know what kind of courses to take —we have a guidance counselor in Cristen, and she's going to help you. Dana is like a life counsellor—just know that I'm living proof of doing the work, of taking a big leap, and I mean just to put a little emphasis on the word *leap* that I took. We moved into our new, very expensive house in the middle of October, and then I turned to Dave and I go, "Hey, so I'm gonna just do this full time. Okay, we're just gonna risk it." But here we are. And you know, he's really supportive, even though he's probably clenching his little fingers, he believes in what we're doing too.

So, I believe in you and everybody else believes in you too! We're here for you if you need us in any way. The last thing I want to say is, oh no, two things. Cristen AKA Shiva Raine has been putting polls on the Facebook group. If you're in the Facebook group, please, please, please partake in those because they're really going to be helpful for us as far as like how we schedule the workshops.

I'm also going to be putting out a request for frequently asked questions. If there are things that you're just not sure of, please share those questions. Anything would be really,

really helpful. Just random questions that I can answer on the website would be great.

Okay, and then the last thing is Dana Sardano wrote a book! It's called *Ten Recommandments for Personal Empowerment*. It's phenomenal! When I went into Alcoholics Anonymous and I did the 12 steps—and I did them with my whole heart—everything changed for me. I thought that the 12 steps should be taught in high school in health class, and we should all learn how to see life this way. Well, that just scratched the surface to what *Ten Recs* does. It is seriously like a beautiful and expressive and informative guide on how to have personal freedom. I believe in this book so much. It's almost like charter documents of Uniquely U. They are so synonymous. We're going to be giving away Dana's audiobook to the first 300 students to , exclusively available on Uniquely U. It is so amazing! She's even teaching workshops on it. It's just phenomenal!

Also, there's gonna be an awesome book launch party on April 30th at 4pm Eastern Standard Time. Dana is going to be doing a live read from one of the stories, which she's also polling. So if you see a poll from Dana on that help us pick which story to read. Dana's book is launching, April

30th and we are probably launching classes in early June, so it's really, really exciting! It's like her launch is like catalyst to begin enrollment for our workshops.

A lot of amazing things happening and a fun fact about April 30th–for those of you that know me or know my story, you know that I had a miscarriage, and I lost a baby. His name was Joshua, and I lost him on December 3rd, but he was supposed to be born April 30th. I just love the synergy and the connections, and I just love seeing his little angelic hand in everything. So, there's something really beautiful about that, too.

That's so Joshua. Ok, that was weird (awkward chuckle). I just feel so weird doing these videos.

Anyway, I just wanted to catch up with you guys, and for those of you who are in our Facebook group and haven't had a chance to interact or interject, please say "Hi" and introduce yourselves. Become an active member of our community because we are all in this together.

We are one. We welcome you. Feel free to ask questions. You can privately message me, Dana, Cristen (AKA Shiva Raine) if you need anything or if you're curious about anything. The website is currently under construction, so you can still go to FindUniquelyU.com if you want to join the mailing list because we'll probably be doing some personal reach out and really connect with people there.

So, that's that for now. I just wanted to send you guys an update and say "Hi", and I miss you, and I love you, and I am excited for all of us, and I hope that everything is going beautifully in your life right now, and you know, just all that good stuff. Peace out!"

20 days later...

A Personal Update

Sent: Wed, Apr 20, 2022, at 11:58 PM

Second Recommandment:
I shalt not become entrenched in my emotions.

From the book *Ten Recommandments for Personal Empowerment*
by Dana Sardano

Hello Friends,

It has been a hot minute since I've written some musings for you, and while I am not quite ready to make the BIG announcement as promised in my last Uniquely U. Update (which IS coming so soon!), I do miss this opportunity to share my experiences with you because doing so helps me see me from your perspective, providing a different view of the situations I grow through so I can learn and "level up", as they say :)

This past weekend, my family and I experienced what was simply the most terrifying experience of our lives to date. Thanks to all the angels and saints, it was not a *tragic* experience. [*Everyone is fine. Everyone is safe. Everyone is whole.* I am going to include things like this every now and again because this is the dialogue I need to have as I recount and remember.]

I'll try to sum it up as unemotionally and detached as I can. On Saturday (Easter Eve), we were driving home from a quick little vacation in Pennsylvania. After a long nap, Christian woke up just as we were getting into Staten Island, and he cried that his teeth were hurting him. Not thinking much of it, I tried to distract him by saying I would hold my phone from the front seat so he could watch videos. I turned around after not having heard a response from him and realized that he was not breathing [*he was safe, we just didn't know what was happening at the time*].

He was staring straight at Mattie, but he was listless [*he was safe.*] I pulled him out of his car seat as Dave pulled over to the side of the highway and Mattie called 911. Christian was unresponsive but his heart was beating. We had no idea if he was choking or what [*he was safe, he was okay, we didn't know so of course it was absolutely terrifying.*] Dave realized he was breathing, and what felt like within both seconds and an eternity, a highway patrolman came up to us and calmed me down. He realized that Christian was having a seizure and was really okay and was actually slowly coming to. I don't know what that patrolman said—his presence was reassuring, and his energy told my energy that there was no reason to panic. He put Christian on the front seat of our truck and was talking to him, and then had Dave talk to him, and Christian made a little moan sound, moved his eyes, and took the tiniest sips of water. At that point, I grabbed Mattie and told her he was fine and safe, and we burst into tears of relief and stress. The FDNY EMT was just the most amazing person ever—I wish I grabbed these people's names— but they all calmed us down and helped us get through this. There was no judgement, only understanding of how this must have been for us to go through. We were taken to the Staten

Island Northwell Health Hospital where we posted up for twelve hours waiting for Christian's heart rate to go down [*he was dehydrated, not dying, he was safe. miraculous water was all he needed.*] We were again surrounded by angelic nurses who were so good with Christian, and me (I was likely the worst patient, asking thousands of questions.)

We learned that Christian had a Febrile Seizure, which is typically brought on by a fever that comes on super-fast. He must have gone from 98 to 103 in minutes. It is most common in children ages 1–6 particularly when there is a family history of them. There weren't any seizures in my family, but Dave's mom told us that all her kids had them when they were young [*one and done is the mantra!*] I have never seen anyone seize, let alone a child, and it really looks like they are dying before your eyes [*he was safe, he was safe*], but now that I know that this is a common reaction to rapidly onsetting super high fevers, I am just going to walk around with children's Motrin in a holster on my hip!

I partly tell this story to serve as a public service announcement to all parents/ caregivers with young children. If Christian has another seizure, the protocol is to make sure he is safe by laying him on his side where he can't harm himself, call 911 and let him just get through it. Oh, and don't put anything in their mouths [*we didn't know you weren't supposed to do that, I thought he was choking on something or his tongue, which now we know can't physically happen.*] He may not breathe for a few insane moments, but he will be okay. The freakin' Mayo Clinic says to call 911 after five minutes of this, but I say call the second it happens because having the support of paramedics who can help from a detached and experienced point of view is a lifesaver.

One of the benefits of being best friends with someone as brilliant and insightful and articulate as Dana (twat punches and all) is that I get first glimpses of her work (such as her upcoming published book *Ten Recommandments for Personal Empowerment*) and a direct line to her guidance and support any time. Dana was the one I called from the hospital because I knew she would talk me off the ledge. When I said something to the effect of, *"I am not going to get over this,"* she said something like, and I paraphrase because I was paralyzed from the trauma, *"So you've already decided that, huh? No, that is not what is going to happen. You are going to recognize that this was a terrifying experience that happened already and you are going to focus on the fact that every-one is safe, everyone is okay, and you are going to move forward and not fall back."* [*I shalt not become entrenched in my emotions.*]

It is now Wednesday, and I am so happy to say that Christian is perfectly perfect, albeit a little grumpy and defiant, which is my 'fault' because while my words and maybe actions say "I'm all good, phew, we made it through that crazy experience!" my energy is still on high alert. And the minute anyone tells me how strong I am being, I start to cry. Go figure!

I had a realization earlier that I was getting stressed about not being able to work. What Dana teaches us to do in the Second Recommandment is to listen to our Emotional Guidance System. (Dana is going to be so proud of me because I read this book last year when she wrote it, but dude...it WORKS!)

I asked myself,

"What am I really stressed about because I know the work will get done when it gets done and there is no reason to stress. Oh, it's jealousy because Dave gets to go to work, and Mattie gets to be out with their friends and I get to sit here agonizing over whether Christian is going to start seizing again. And if I were able to go to work and distract myself and let someone else be responsible for him, I would get a momentary reprieve from the fear, but the fear would still be here. So instead of slapping on a Band-aide, I am going to appreciate this gift of being with Christian and looking fear in the face and telling it to fuck off. I am going to be as completely in the present as I can be, and when my mind drifts, I am going to gently bring it back to the present, because now is where the magic is. NOW is where I want to be always."

Almost immediately when I went through this, I felt only compassion for myself, Dave, Mattie, and Christian. Christian and I wound up having a great night, and he went to bed with such ease. At least for today, doing 'the work' of healing is working.

No doubt, the memories are still very vivid, and to avoid crumbling into an abyss of anguish when they appear in my brain, I say things like, *"thank God we were where we were when it happened"* and *"now we know what this looks like and what to do (empowered, not powerless)"* and *"Christian was safe. WE just didn't know what was happening, and that is okay."* I am looking for the gratitude in every nook and cranny because, as my good friend Roger says,

"This is YOUR shit. Eat your shit. LOVE your shit. Transmute that shit into LOVE and you will raise the vibration of the planet."

I don't know about you, but if I can turn this experience into something that raises our global frequency, I am all GAME-ON! [*Christian is and always was safe. My family is whole. This was not tragic, just terrifying.*]

And that is all I have to say about that. I hope this helps some of you see your way out of whatever darkness you might find yourself in by shining a light on what it could be. To badly quote Dana one more time, *"This is YOUR story. YOU choose what happens next."* I will see you all VERY soon when we open the doors to Uniquely U.!!! Much love to you all. I miss you and appreciate you so much.

If you haven't reserved your spot yet, please join **Dana's Live Book Launch Event for *Ten Recommandments for Personal Empowerment* on Saturday, April 30th, 4–6pm EST,** moderated by yours truly. It is going to be a magically delicious time!

Christian enjoyed a much-deserved ice pop on Easter morning when we returned home from the ER.

Uniquely Yours,

Angela DiMarco, *Founder + CEO*

Two months later...

Uniquely U. Update #52 (OMG!)

Sent: Tues, June 14, 2022, at 9:24 PM

"This is the time to remember
'Cause it will not last forever
These are the days to hold on to
But we won't although we'll want to

This is the time
But time is gonna change
You've given me the best of you
But now I need the rest of you"

Lyrics from the song *This is the Time* by Billy Joel

Hello, My Friends!

Guess what? It's almost here!
Uniquely U. is about to be born into the world!

How's it been going? I have missed you!!! For those of you who have been following along for the past year, I had paused my weekly emails (you're welcome!) to go below ground and build this platform. Well, it is with my greatest pleasure to announce that on Monday, June 20th, Uniquely U. will be opening the gates for the very first time, and we want you to be among the first to walk around and take in that new car smell!

As our way of thanking you for being a part of our (my) journey this past year, we are offering you a first-in-line opportunity to reserve a seat in any workshop/s that interest you before we open the gates to the general public on June 27th.

June 20th-June 26th is "Friends + Fam Week"

You will be able to register for any of the amazing workshops we have lined up for an additional 10% off, which is a total of 20% savings (that's like free money!!) On Monday, June 20th, I will share the important information you need, like links and coupons and all that jazz, and that, my friends, will be the very last personal email I write to the Uniquely U. community.

I mean, there may be others but nothing like what we have shared here together. For those of you who've read at least some of my emails, you know how personal and deep and honest I've gotten with you. And even though this may seem like a one-way street, it didn't feel that way. Even if you didn't comment back, I felt your support and genuine care, and for that, I will be forever grateful for the opportunity to grow through this experience of building a business from a seed of an idea to something so in-credibly beautiful and inspiring.

This journey of starting Uniquely U. has been nothing short of extraordinary! The idea plopped in my brain after taking Victor Oddo's workshop in the fall of 2020 with some amazing friends. Then, when I told Dana Sardano, my SDT sorority sister from USF in Tampa about the idea in November 2020, the idea became a firmly planted seed, and I began to embody the Uniquely U. concept. First, I wrote it all down, every detail. Then I created a visual presentation and just took little baby steps, trying to eat one piece of candy at a time.

Very early on, people helped me find my footing. I ran a beta Brand DNA Workshop in February 2021 out of the travel office I rented by the hour on Tuesday nights to prove out my concept, and the old friends and new ones that joined me for those four weeks gave me the strength and fortitude to move forward—you guys are still and always will be the 'In(augural) Crowd'—our experience was so, so special to me!

Dana's daily coaching and pushing and twat-punching guided me to make changes and choices that helped me discover who I really am, what my unique qualities are, and what really makes me tick. Then she did something so incredibly awe-inspiring that still rocks me to my core...she handed me the big, fat capital I needed to quit my secure, albeit a bit boring day job to make this dream a reality. Dana's unwavering faith in me became the mirror I needed for me to have unwavering faith in myself.

So, not just because my you-know-what is sore from her punches, not just because she handed me a buttload of money out of her mutandi drawer, not just because she invested so much time in caring for me and my family while she was (SUCCESSFULLY) growing back her thyroid (more on that in her third book, *Beyond the Ten, Decoding the Woo Woo*), and not just because she is so brilliant and has shaped our U-Instructor training program to be so freaking amazing—but because of all these reasons combined, Dana is officially and deservingly my Co-Founder, my partner, my wonder twin, my bestie, my Co-Creator. We would not be ready to fly if not for her.

In October 2021, Dave and I bought our dream house, and just a few weeks after we moved in, I told him I *had* to quit my day job and do this. With an expensive mortgage and two kids to feed, this of course came across as a very reasonable decision, right? So, on Dec. 3rd, 2021 (my angel baby Joshua's Day), I left that full time job and 25+ long career in marketing to build Uniquely U. full time. I've been all in ever since, and now I can't see myself doing anything else. I shift my work area around our house daily because I am so incredibly in love with my home, my backyard (my garden!)—I have created that coveted work/life balance and my days are 99% angst free (I'll always be a work in progress—that is what makes this life so fun and interesting!)

So here we are, folks! It is safe to say that I was apprehensive, sure, but having the most amazing rock stars around me and on my team has made me feel that *everything* is possible. Cristen left her career of 25+ years to join us back in March. HER faith and ability to see the possibilities and to take such a huge leap of faith puts even more steam in my engine! Rob...gees, Rob is a freakin' nerd genius, and I couldn't love my unofficial brother in law anymore. He can solve the greatest puzzles and make it seem easy! And Tricia, Girl, you're most recent to the party, but I have never seen anyone work as hard and learn as fast as you do, all with an elegant calmness that rubs all over me in the right ways! Cheerleaders Mattie, Dave, Christian (who forces me to stop and appreciate the tiniest things on a daily basis), Mat, Aunt Ang and Mom, you guys sure know how to build up a girl when she needs it most!

U-Instructors! All of you are just the freakin' cat's meow! I can't wait to watch you guys shine brighter than the sun—I am forever and ever and ever grateful that you signed up for the unknown and stuck with us through the learning curves. You helped shape our Ready-Set-Teach! training process more than you could ever know, making it smoother sailing for all U-Ins who follow. You are truly pioneers!

And then there is Scopic (sigh)—y'all make my heart flutter! Megi, Hanjo and the rest of the amazing, magical digital development team are, as Tina Turner says, "Simply the best!" You are all just so talented and such authentically wonderful humans. Our partnership is unlike any other. We are and will be successful because of you guys! We are in this together through and through!

So, my friends, thank you for allowing me all these pixels to pontificate on why I am so in love with this moment in time with all the people I am surrounded by. Come Monday, everything is going to be different. We will be on the other side of this moment. So today, I just want to revel in all its glory. We have all worked really, really hard, but we have had a blast building this, and **I can't WAIT** for you guys to see what we made here!

It feels like it's Christmas Eve, and I've wrapped up Uniquely U. with a giant, purple bow and put it under the tree and am waiting for you to wake up and open it!

Please take a moment on Monday to register for a free account on the platform, because that is the only way I will be able to stay connected to you. This email list you are on is officially being archived. Of course, I will be reachable at this email address anytime you need me, but it would mean the world to me if you could continue your support by fueling my tank with your beautiful energy. I will be sharing ways for you to help spread the word as well. All I desire as we launch the platform is to provide awareness that we exist. Whoever aligns with us will join us, but they just need to know we are here.

And with that, I will end this very long, on par email with one final message:

```
With all my heart,
      thank you.
```

It's been an amazing journey so far, and we've only just begun!

Uniquely Yours,
Angela DiMarco, *Founder, President + CEO*

Epilogue

Thurs, December 22, 2022

Geesh, some of that was hard for me to read!—not so much reliving of the painful experiences but more so my almost annoying optimism, especially in the beginning.

Throughout my whole life, I have always considered myself an open book, one who wears her heart on her sleeve. Yet while there was not a lick of *intentional* inauthenticity in any of those emails (I always meant every word I said—even the super effusive words held truth), I could see the protective layers hiding my lack of self-worth, my inability to get my needs met, and to even trust those closest to me to meet my needs. My insecurities were evident in those early days.

In retrospect, my true intention behind sharing these emails was to get the attaboys I so desired, to prove my worth in bringing a new business into the world and to garner support that I always seemed to have to fight for. At the same time, I also truly loved bringing people along for the ride.

Because spilling my guts was my modus operandi, it served me well to publicly journal my adventures in new entrepreneurship. Every single person mentioned in this story taught me something about myself—from how to *not* eat all the candy at one time (*patience, wait and see,* and *let things play out* are the new normal) to protecting my energy and setting boundaries.

Throughout these past two years, I have rediscovered how truly special I am and to *embrace what makes me special,* for we all have something special to offer the world. I was just so bogged down from the weight of allowing other people to define me that I never truly realized what I was capable of.

My initial wake-up call came from Joshua, but I'll admit that I hit the snooze button a few times. It was really at around the events of September 2021 (Update #34) that my desire to help the world (and unknowingly myself) overcame my desire to hide under my insecurities. It was one thing to experience the shift in real time, but it is really cool to see the evidence of that shift in my writing.

Of all the gifts this journey has bestowed upon me, the greatest of all is my personal empowerment—now knowing who I am and not only discerning that which brings me contentment, peace, and joy over unease, angst, and fear but also doing the work necessary to keep my pendulum center and steady.

Just after the last update #52 in June 2022, I had a falling out with my entire family—my mother, my aunt, my brothers and sisters—all of them. In one fell swoop, they were gone from my life. It was quite jarring, but it was my choice to firmly hold a boundary that I set, resulting in leashes being removed, masks being dropped, and decades of unspoken truths being spoken. No longer wearing blinders, I was finally able to see how toxic those relationships had been. So, on the day that we officially launched Uniquely U., June 27th, 2022, I officially cleaned house of all the relationships that no longer served me and started with a clean slate.

This was an extremely painful experience. If you saw the movie *The Sixth Sense*, you can imagine how I was feeling in the subsequent months after divorcing my family. Looking back on my earliest memories, I could now see with clarity all the moments that contributed to my many layers of self-protection, revealing shocks of *it was all right there all along* at every turn. These consistent snapshots of truth have made it easier to stand my ground because we all know that when we break up with someone, it is never going to be different the next time, unless someone offers the olive branch, but even then, the discernment tool needs to remain sharp.

To re-read these emails in their entirety as a bystander, I am honestly so proud of who and where I am at this point in my life. My intention was to share my adventures in starting a business as a first-time entrepreneur, but really, rediscovering myself was an adventure of a completely different kind.

Thank you for joining me on this journey. If you want to see how things play out, join me in real time on FindUniquelyU.com. I'd love to connect with you.

About the Author

Prior to creating Uniquely U., Angela spent her formative years working at well-known advertising agencies in NYC. Over many late nights, Angela helped in creating on-brand, effective work across all mediums, gaining invaluable experience working with huge, national clients.

It was with a desire to work directly with clients as partners, an intuitive knack for solving strategic and visual challenges, and the passion to help small businesses grow that Angela left the world of big agencies and began collaborating with like-minded creative entrepreneurs.

In 2010, Angela laid the foundation for *The Thirsty Creative Group*, a unique agency platform that is equal parts traditional freelance and white-labeled creative services. Angela has sat as the Executive Creative Director for small agencies with big clients and has led diverse teams and vendor partners in building meaningful brand experiences for customers.

In 2017, Angela went client-side and joined a manufacturing company as their first in-house Marketing Director. The pandemic, however, has led her to get back to her passion of wanting to help "the little guy" by making guidance accessible to those who long to rediscover themselves. As such, Uniquely U. was born.

Uniquely U. is an uncommon commonplace that brings opportunity for teachers and students with the core essence of finding and nurturing that unique, differentiating factor, and shining a light on it as a personal brand. Angela has been known throughout her career as the "Connector" and Uniquely U. is the ultimate platform for her to bring people together who can spark ideas and set dream-achieving action into motion.

After 'finding herself' at University of South Florida at Tampa, Angela transferred to SUNY Farmingdale and graduated second in her class, receiving a BA in Visual Communications. She has since been creating compelling commercial art for clients in the marketing/advertising industry.

In November 2022, with co-collaborator Dana Sardano, Angela co-founded *Phenom Publishing* and sits as the Chief Creative Officer. She collaborates with Phenom's authors to create a design for their books that expresses the promise and premise of the experience the reader will have between the covers.

Want to stay in touch? Connect with Angela at:

FindUniquelyU.com or **Phenom-Publishing.com**, or catch an episode of ***Cuddle Talk with Angela & Dana*** on YouTube.

PUBLISHING

If you have passion in your heart and a voice for your spirit, then you should have the freedom to share it with others. When you uplift and inspire another through *your* stories of *your* greatness and *your* resilience then you are in your own right a phenom.

Phenom Publishing was created by Dana Sardano and Angela DiMarco for those of you who have something special to offer, something created from your soul and delivered through your heart, something that is yearning to be heard.

Phenom recognizes that within we are *all* phenoms, and through our creativity, we *all* have the ability to change our inner worlds which ultimately changes the world around us. Dana and Angela have begun by sharing their individual stories, and they encourage you to share yours so that humanity can unite and thrive in its phenomenal collective story.

If you have something to share and the voice to share it and are seeking a platform to share it on, join the movement and become the voice of the people.

Become a phenom.

Editors@Phenom-Publishing.com

Made in the USA
Middletown, DE
09 January 2023